MR. RICH

VS.

THE JONESES

Living Within Your Means

J.J. Logan

First Printing, 2014

ISBN: 978-1500433963

Library of Congress Control Number: 2014912291

CreateSpace Independent Publishing Platform, North Charleston, SC

Contents

Preface

We all wish for more money, fewer bills and financial stability. How often have you fantasized about what to do with lottery winnings if only you had the winning numbers? How often have you longed for a mysterious long lost relative to send loads of cash your way? If you're like me and many others I know, you have had these thoughts and more for quite a while. If one of these scenarios has come true, congratulations! For everyone else, this book is here to serve as a guide on your journey to living within your means.

I am a husband and father of two with a slight obsession over money, investing, reducing debt and of course discounts! After all, who doesn't get a rush out of finding the best possible deal on anything they buy? In my case, it has become a way of life and I'm excited to pass all of this knowledge on to my kids, family and you. From spending and saving habits to income ideas and easy to find freebies, I hope to educate everyone out there who is struggling to make ends meet. With this knowledge in hand, financial stability is within your grasp.

Introduction

Young or old, rich or poor there are 3 primary ways to improve your finances. Spend less, make more and save more. If it were really that easy though, you probably wouldn't be reading this book. Within each of these concepts are many individual methods that may or may not work for you. Many people can give advice on how they live their lives, but it is up to each of us to determine the methods that work best for our particular situations.

This book will detail all of the tricks I have gathered over the years that appear to work well, are easy to achieve and will apply to the average person. I will also include some extra pieces of information such as forms, formulas and cheap and healthy home cooking recipes for those of you interested in eating out a bit less. If you feel you have already mastered an area, feel free to skip forward but be warned...you might miss an important tip!

1 – The Joneses

Have you ever heard the phrase "keeping up with the Joneses"? Of course everyone has, but have you ever really sat down to think about what that means? It means we look at those around us wishing to have what they have. It could be something as large as a house or as small as an iPod, as prestigious as a high ranking job or as common as a greener yard. Whatever the reason, we all have a deep desire to acquire that which we do not currently have.

Speaking of a greener yard, let's visit another common phrase – "The grass is always greener on the other side of the fence." Taken literally, you could very well wish your lawn could look as nice as the neighbor's. But more often than not the saying refers to the feeling that everything would be better if only I had *blank*. Feel free to fill in the blank with whatever comes to mind, but I'm sure you are beginning to notice some similarities between the two phrases.

So, we all want to keep up with the Joneses and the grass always appears greener elsewhere. Let us delve deeper into how the Joneses live and how green that other grass really is. Before the Great Recession, I would repeatedly ask myself and my wife the same questions about those around us with larger houses, fancier cars and plenty of pricey toys.

"How does everyone in our neighborhood afford such large houses AND expensive cars?"

"Do they really make that much more money than we do?"

As it turns out, the answer to the second question was "no" and the answer to the first was "a lot of them are living beyond their means". Of course at the time this fact was not obvious but then the Great Recession hit and it suddenly became crystal clear. Houses all throughout my neighborhood were up for sale or in foreclosure while articles hit the news daily about how in debt the average American was.

During this time I discovered a huge difference between what I considered rich and wealthy. The rich are typically viewed as those that currently have a lot. A big house, fancy cars and all kinds of expensive things would qualify someone for the title of "rich". But if all of those items were purchased on credit, those people might just be drowning in debt, own nothing and live with huge monthly payments.

This is when reality began to sink in. There was a sudden realization that a lot of people in America do live beyond their means, many more than I had ever expected. This means a lot of people are simply spending more than they earn in an unsustainable way. Eventually debts come due and if you are unable to pay them, disaster strikes.

That led to my next revelation. If the Joneses were real they would be broke, facing foreclosure, drowning in debt and filing for bankruptcy. Simply put, that is a horrible lifestyle that no one should strive to achieve yet they do. As I soon realized, the difference between my way of life and those around me was that while they were driving expensive cars, buying the latest gadgets and living in big, expensive houses, I was paying off debts, increasing savings and preparing just in case I lost my job. Apparently my grass was greener after all.

The truth is, most financially stable people are not the ones driving fancy cars, wearing suits and dresses with fancy jewelry and (insert your idea of a rich person here). They are most likely the family down the street driving used cars in a house that fits them perfectly that cooks meals at home and dresses like...well...the family down the street! As you'll see later in the book, we'll refer to this type of person as "Mr. Rich".

You see, as it turns out all those expensive items do cost a lot. Some of them even cost a lot to own and maintain or create stress once they are yours. Have you ever thought about how much insurance costs on an expensive sports car? How about how much less that brand new boat is worth the minute you put it in the water? Do you really want to use those expensive dishes knowing how much it will cost if you break one and need to replace it? How much do your neighbors with the bright green lawn have to pay a lawn service each month?

My best advice to you at this point is that the grass is not always greener and it should not matter to you what others have. Enjoy what is yours, put thought into all of your purchases and live with the knowledge that money will not actually burn a hole in your pocket if not spent quickly.

2 – Change Your Mindset

In order to gain financial stability a mindset change will need to occur. It will be a completely new way of life. All aspects of how you view income, expenses, wealth and possessions must be adapted to how the world really works rather than how marketing teams want consumers to view it. I am sorry to say that skipping one morning Latte is not going to make a huge difference by itself and finding a buy one, get one free coupon for an item you will never use is not a great deal. The good news is, with a little knowledge both of those items are a great start to what could blossom into a profitable future.

As a college student in the mid 90s with little financial experience beyond that learned from grade school, jobs and a personal savings account, the realities of the world were cold and unforgiving. That first trip to the store to purchase toiletries was my first huge and unexpected reality check. Who knew how much money parents actually dish out each month for items that seemed so insignificant? When every purchase comes out of a very limited supply of cash with no parental help your view and use of money quickly begins to change. Every purchase becomes a balancing act, a give and take. With $5 in your pocket, is eating out for lunch at a popular fast food restaurant or buying soap for the shower and ramen noodles on sale at the local discount store a better use of funds?

This is something everyone must come to terms with in their own way and it is the very first step on the way to financial stability. This mindset change allows you to separate wants from needs, determine a priority of those items then spend limited funds in the most appropriate way.

If all transactions were cash based with no alternatives, decisions on purchase priorities would be much easier as choices would have immediate and visible consequences. However there is this little thing called *credit* that changes the game drastically. Along with learning how to properly allocate my limited funds in college came additional lessons taught by a shiny new credit card.

Although credit was a concept I understood, being an 18 year old college student with very little real credit experience tends to allow a credit card to look like free money. With that in mind, I did understand that credit is a loan that must be paid back, preferably at the end of the month in order to avoid finance charges. This fact seems simple but as I was soon to find out it is much more difficult than it appears.

The first setback appeared when my car broke down and needed a new alternator. Being young and relatively inexperienced the concept of an emergency fund had not been ingrained into my mind. Although an understanding of how to properly spend limited funds was beginning to truly sink in, saving funds for a future unknown expense was still a foreign concept. That left an unexpected car repair expense with no funds to pay for it. With very few options it was time for credit to come to the rescue!

That was the beginning of what would grow to be $4,000 of debt on one credit card. Although the initial limit was only $1,000, never missing a payment and staying under the allocated limit encouraged my credit card company to increase the maximum available credit. After all, I was a profitable and reliable credit user that welcomed the increase. But as time went on it became easier and easier to buy something on the card while only making the minimum monthly payment. At one point I actually remember waiting for the minimum monthly payment to hit the account in order to charge something else.

This is a widespread issue that many families deal with and a lesson that took many years for me to learn. Spending beyond your means via credit is an unsustainable process that increases debt which must be repaid at some point in the future. If not paid in full each month, interest on debt accumulates making the balance more difficult to pay off. Eventually this pattern will lead to default or worse, bankruptcy.

Thankfully during this time of increasing debt I was in college working towards a degree in Business Computer Systems which I hoped would allow the generation of much more income in order to pay off the debt and further my career. But even that had its downside. Due to the cost of college tuition, debt was slowly increasing via student loans eventually growing to $20,000. As a 22 year old male with a total of $24,000 in debt the future was looking grim. Without realizing it a lesson was being learned that would change my life forever. Spending less and making more began to consume my thoughts. I began looking for additional ways to generate income such as picking up extra part time shifts, looking for jobs that paid just a bit better as well as trying desperately to find ways to spend less each week. In doing so, I managed to pay every monthly bill, increase my credit score and learn several valuable lessons that will be explained in detail throughout this book.

This story does have a happy ending. After learning to cut costs as low as possible, keep debt from growing and value any income stream, I graduated and found my first web development job. A college level job provided a much higher income than any job before and the lessons learned throughout that difficult time created a determination to properly take advantage of the increased income. By living at home with parents, continuing the frugal lifestyle learned during late college years and paying as much extra as was possible each month towards that $24,000, I managed to become debt free in less than two years. This began a lifestyle of living beneath my means, continuing to cut expenses whenever possible, saving for retirement and paying off debts quickly.

If you have ever been in debt or are currently in debt you are probably wondering "Ok yeah this is great in theory but how do I actually start changing my mindset?" Well, a perfect place to start on a path to financial stability is to come up with goals. Whether it is to skip that morning latte once a week, cook an additional meal at home or put $100 aside into savings each month, by writing these down and revisiting them each week you will find yourself looking at finances a bit differently. This shift will expand in time to include every financial decision made. Start small and build on that progress each month. Next, expand those goals and target issues specific to your situation.

How often have you received some unexpected income which was immediately spent on a frivolous purchase? A few examples could be a tax return, an extra paycheck if you are paid biweekly rather than monthly or a gift of cash in a card for your birthday or a holiday. Worse yet, how often have you spent an expected sum of money before even receiving it? The most common time I witness this is with tax returns for the previous year.

By changing your mindset on how that money is used, your first impulse could be to put an unexpected sum in savings, set it aside for a family vacation or begin saving for something you desire. By not spending it right away or before it is even in hand you have successfully avoided a common trap many people fall into and have taken another step towards financial stability and living within your means. Remember, money will not actually burn a hole in your pocket. It can sit there content for quite some time!

As shown in my college experience, using a credit card to make a purchase you could not otherwise afford is a danger everyone could be susceptible to. Emergencies do happen and it is not always possible to be completely prepared to deal with them so a minor debt increase is acceptable. However, this should be an emergency situation only, not a regular occurrence.

Do you ever find yourself buying something using a credit card even if you do not have the money in an account to pay for that purchase? Put that on your list of items to stop doing. Credit cards should be for convenience or emergencies only, getting paid off every month with money available in a checking or savings account. By remembering this each time that card is used you have taken another step.

If you have trouble keeping credit spending in check try putting a sticky note on each credit card with the a question like "Do I really need this?" or "Do I have cash in the bank for this?" or "Put me back! The light, it burns!" written on top. Whatever catches your attention will do.

If married, dating seriously or have someone else to share finances with there is a bit more to the financial picture than just how *you* spend and save. This other person must be on the same page with a similar financial mindset. If one spouse saves while the other spends, progress will be hard to come by and the spender will usually win. This also requires a deep level of trust in a relationship as both parties must be completely honest with one another. Many relationships can fail due to monetary stressors or dishonesty about money. It could be that one has a hidden spending problem or that neither party has a clear understanding of the overall income and expenses. Whatever the case may be, open discussion, honestly and a combined clear understanding of your goals will go a long way in financial stability relationship strength.

The last and greatest realization on the path to changing your mindset will be the difference between what you view as "rich" versus your view on "wealthy". Those two terms typically conjure up very personal images that could be the same or similar. Think about those two words for a minute and note the differences in what each of them creates.

The first time I did this exercise, rich meant having a lot of money or being able to display riches to the rest of the world. The image was that of a young, flashy executive driving an expensive sports car. Wealth on the other hand conjured images of an old man, comfortable and confident, relaxing on a beach without a care in the world. To this day those two images still come to mind when comparing the two phrases.

Breaking those images down to find what they were rooted in, I found the difference of rich versus wealthy to me was that of instant cash versus net worth or instant riches versus long term wealth. The rich young executive lives life in the fast lane and displays what he has to everyone. He is the epitome of the Joneses, possessing many items while living in debt. But the wealthy old man has it all figured out and is able to relax because of the resulting wealth of a life of wise decisions.

Net worth is actually a very important concept to understand. This term is used to describe how much money an individual is worth once everything they own is added up and everything they owe is subtracted. The calculation is as follows:

Net worth = assets – liabilities

If the Joneses have a large number of expensive items with very large loans, their net worth may very well be 0. Recognizing the difference and separation between instant riches with debt and long term wealth will make a mindset change much easier to accomplish. A long term vision of wealth will then help you find the path that leads there.

3 – Entitlement

For some reason it has become common in recent years for many people to believe they deserve goods, services or privileges without providing anything in return. This concept is referred to as entitlement. To be honest, this change in behavior baffles me. What causes an individual to think they deserve something for nothing?

Since my teenage years it was well known that if I wanted something, it must be earned. Whether that meant doing chores in order to receive an allowance, babysitting to receive spending money or doing homework to receive a good grade it was obvious the responsibility sat squarely on my shoulders. I embraced that responsibility and worked hard in order to achieve or acquire all I desired.

While not everything desired was within my grasp, I accepted that fact and used it as an internal drive to work harder. Additional effort put forth into something resulted in a better outcome and a pattern of hard work resulted in success.

Fast forwarding to adult life, I understand that homeownership is a privilege for those willing to save, maintain a good credit score and accept the responsibility of a long term loan. If not taken seriously, a lack of that responsibility will result in a financial disaster. Yet all too often I see others barely able to make ends meet assuming they too should be able to own a home regardless of whether they are financially capable of doing so. This appears to be viewed as an American right rather than something to strive for and one day achieve.

Technology gadgets are another common area I see many people spending frivolously beyond their means. It seems the current trend is that everyone wants to own an iPad or iPhone (www.apple.com). While it is widely accepted that those are nice products, they too are a privilege, not a right. The reality is, if you do not have $600 (or current market price) for an iPad you do not deserve it. This is a luxury item that must be saved up for and funded from some form of income.

While attempting to change your mindset and prepare for a more promising financial future, please remember to avoid any feelings of entitlement. If something is desired, it must be earned through hard work and planning. Remember, while the best things in life are free, those you desire may not be.

4 – Spend Less Than You Earn

Spending less than you earn seems a simple enough concept but time and time again I see well meaning individuals spending a bit more than they should. The best way to begin on a journey to consistently spend less than you earn is to create a budget. This provides an overview of your entire current financial situation which will become the basis for all future actions.

The initial goal of this budget should not be to force you to give up everything you enjoy or to make your income and expenses match. Rather, the goal should simply be to find out exactly how much is earned and where it all gets spent. The most important part of this process is honesty in order to get an accurate picture so when in doubt overestimate expenses and underestimate income. It is better to end up with more money left over at the end of the month than the budget expects than to be surprised by a shortfall.

When creating this budget be sure to include every form of income after taxes, every major expense and every recurring bill. For smaller items, try not to get too detailed right off the bat. Instead, spend a few weeks determining how much is spent on things like eating out, morning coffee, gas, tolls, groceries and anything else you can think of. Once the specifics numbers have been determined over that short time frame, add them up and come up with a general estimate that can be used in the budget. Similar to dieting, too much effort all at once can cause a crash which sets you back farther rather than increasing progress. By using an average estimate on smaller items, plenty of time and energy will be saved that can be better spent elsewhere.

If married, be sure your spouse is involved in this budget. Both parties must include every form of income and every expense in order for this exercise to be effective. Accuracy is extremely important at this point and a team can be far more productive than an individual. In addition to ensuring accuracy, a budget in a family takes constant effort from everyone involved so once again, honestly is extremely important.

Do not fear including splurge expenses. Everyone enjoys a good splurge purchase so it makes sense to account for that rather than pretend it does not exist. When the final budget is created, if there are still items you do not want to break out into individual line items, simply consolidate them into a single "Splurge" item with a correctly estimated monthly amount.

Since expenses are typically more difficult to consolidate than income, please see the following chart for assistance. Add in any items missing from the list in the blank lines at the bottom.

Budget	
Expense	**Amount**
Mortgage #1	
Mortgage #2	
Home Phone	
Cell Phone	
Internet	
TV	
Auto Loan	
Auto Insurance	
Electricity - Utility	
Gas - Utility	
Water - Utility	
Gym Membership	
Website Subscriptions	
Gas - Auto	
Groceries	
Fast Food	
Life Insurance	
Homeowner's Association Dues	
Medical Prescriptions	
Cigarettes	
Alcohol	
TOTAL	**$**

With a hard copy of income and expenses in hand, use the following formula to determine whether you are currently living within your means:

INCOME (after taxes) – EXPENSES = Extra/Shortfall

If the result is a positive number, congratulations you are currently on track to spend less than you earn and live within your means! If the result is a negative number this indicates you are most likely increasing debt each month. Is the result of this exercise surprising? Is the length of the expense list surprising? In my experience surprise is a common reaction when faced with the realization of where money goes each month. Now, whether the result was extra or a shortfall the next step is to find quick and easy areas to cut spending or save money.

Start by looking for unnecessary recurring monthly expenses. Sometimes we tend to forget how many services we pay for but do not use such as magazine subscriptions, newspapers, gaming subscriptions, movie subscriptions or online subscriptions to websites. If you currently pay extra for premium cable channels that are infrequently watched, cut them out. Do you have a membership to a local health club or workout facility that is rarely used? If so, cancel it and find free ways to exercise outdoors such as walking, running, biking, hiking or simply throwing a ball. If you happen to be paying for a personal trainer at that health club, try finding free online workout videos or articles online about how to get a great workout at home.

Once the obvious extras have been cut out, it is time to find ways to reduce the cost of the remaining bills that were deemed necessary. Although cutting out premium cable channels is a great start, think about just how necessary cable itself really is.

A few years ago my wife and I decided we had finally had enough of paying for 500 channels filled with commercials and nothing good to watch. So, we cautiously agreed to try an experiment by cancelling our cable service and using only streaming Netflix (www.netflix.com) and Hulu (www.hulu.com) for video entertainment. Surprisingly, the result was that we did not miss cable at all and instead enjoyed the variety of instant choices available at our fingertips.

Recently a great deal was available to add cable back to our monthly subscription package so we accepted it. What we found was extremely surprising. Not only had we not missed cable before, now we find ourselves constantly frustrated by the overwhelming number of commercials and lack of quality programming during anything other than prime time. I admit that living cable free might not be for everyone but I was surprisingly happy without it and disappointed when returning to it.

Do you have a smart phone with unlimited minutes, text messaging and data? Review cell phone bills for the last 6 months to see if downgrading to a plan with fewer minutes, fewer texts or less data is a viable option to save money. It might even be possible to go without a smart phone altogether which would save the cost of a data plan.

Speaking of cell phones and smart phones, do your kids have them? Do they actually need them? Think about that question for a few minutes. Most kids will say they "need" whatever the most popular kid in class has. It's the early version of "keeping up with the Joneses". If you do feel a cell phone is necessary, try using a pay as you go type phone in order to reduce expenses and discourage continual use. By comparing wants versus needs and making an informed decision, this might be an easy way to cut costs especially if your kids have unnecessary data plans and smart phones. This can also serve as a learning experience that will help kids avoid trying to keep up with the expensive habits of those around them in the future.

Do you pay for Satellite radio? If so, you might benefit from cancelling it and trying free options such as Pandora (www.pandora.com). If you have internet service at home, check the download and upload speeds for your subscription. If they are higher than you need, feel free to downgrade to a less expensive plan that fits your needs. Do you have a home phone that is actually used? With mobility increasing and constant availability becoming so important, most of the people I know use their home phone rarely at most, instead relying on cell phones for all voice communication. If you fall into that category, consider canceling the home phone service and using a cell phone as a "home" phone.

Many carriers provide package discounts which can add up to quite a bit. Try to consolidate services you currently pay for into as few service providers as is possible in order to receive the maximum possible benefit from these discounts. Cable, internet, home phone and cell phone are 4 services that can easily be combined for a discount from several major providers. Most insurance companies also offer a discount by combining several policies through them.

Once you have cut out both unnecessary monthly expenses as well as cut costs on those you deem necessary, if expenses still outweigh income, it is time to begin cutting what you think are necessities. Take a good hard look at every expense remaining and question whether it is possible to get by without it. Some items cannot be cut out such as utility bills, food or gas but it is possible to conserve and therefore slightly reduce those bills. Beyond that, cuts in actual services will be necessary. It might be difficult as there are quite a few items thought of as necessities which are actually luxuries. For these items the hard truth is if you can't afford it, you can't have it.

5 – Alternative Income

Now that an attempt has been made to reduce costs on easy to cut expenses you may find a few desirable luxury items you wish to purchase or keep a recurring subscription for. In order to do so, an alternative income source must be found in order to increase the Income side of our equation.

INCOME (after taxes) – EXPENSES = Extra/Shortfall

It is not always possible to run out and find a job that pays more than your current position but it never hurts to look. Since that is a more obvious way to tackle the goal of increased income I will leave that to you and instead provide several other less obvious methods.

Have you ever considered picking up a second job? This does not have to mean working 2 full time jobs with night shifts in order to be successful. Try starting out small and see where it takes you. A part time job at a local business working 1 night and 1 weekend day per week might provide all the extra income needed.

Rather than becoming an employee with regular working hours, do you have a valuable skill that others might be willing to pay for on an as needed basis? A few options that might work are mowing lawns, part time local handyman work, filing documents, website design or homemade artwork. The options are endless and based upon the skills you have. Take some time to think about all of the skills obtained throughout your years in this world. You might find more than expected.

Are you married with a stay at home spouse? Consider having both partners work. This could mean one working a full time job while the other works part time or both working full time. This is not necessarily an easy decision so take some time to think about it. If you have children, childcare costs will need to be taken into account. If the income of the 2nd spouse more than offsets the cost of childcare, this could very well be a viable option. If it does not, it would be better to leave the 2nd spouse at home as that will save more money.

Keep in mind the other less tangible costs of a dual income household versus a stay at home spouse. While 2 incomes provide substantially more cash, other areas may suffer. A stay at home spouse can do dishes, laundry, clean, cook, run errands and manage a household much more efficiently than a pair that both work full time. While this does not necessarily equate to a monetary expense, it does involve emotional and physical stress which must be taken into account.

Sell Belongings

Try selling old items you have laying around the house that no longer get regular use. Attics, garages, closets, cabinets and other storage areas can provide quite a few forgotten gems with the ability to provide some additional income. Once you find and organize these items, there are plenty of ways to generate revenue from them.

Websites likes www.ebay.com provide a quick and easy way to list items for sale and receive payment all via the internet. For a local and more personal option try listing your items on www.craigslist.org. Buyers can find your listing online then meet up with you to view and purchase your wares in person. Garage sales are another tried and true method of generating a bit of income. If your community offers a garage sale day, take advantage of it as it will most likely generate much more traffic than a single garage sale would. If not, see if you can convince neighbors to band together for a larger sale that will attract more buyers.

If none of the above methods suit your style, try visiting a local consignment shop. Some will purchase items from you to resell in their shop while others will display your item for a small fee and provide cash once the item sells. Whatever your preference, any of these methods can generate at least a small amount of income.

My personal experience is that these methods are best for generating funds needed to buy a new luxury item, since selling your belongings is obviously not a sustainable source of income. As a matter of fact, I was recently able to save up for and purchase a new television using a combination of all of these methods.

Barter

Beyond just trading cash for items there is an old method of economic activity called bartering. The basic idea is that rather than pay money for something, you trade goods or services with others. This can work great with families or close neighbors. If you have relatives or friends with skills that could help you, offer up your own skills to them in return for theirs. A great example of this could be swapping babysitting duties. By alternating weekends with another family, each couple has an opportunity to get out and about child free every other week.

Speaking of children, try trading gently used child items with family and friends when possible. By passing on clothing, toys, beds or sporting equipment a generous cycle could be created within your family or neighborhood that benefits everyone. If you have a stubborn child that refuses to use anything even remotely related to a "hand me down", try wrapping the items and giving them to your child as a gift. Although seemingly minor, the difference in delivery could change their overall perception of the item.

Share Costs

Have you considered renting out that extra room in your house, condo or apartment? This is obviously something to be careful with as bringing a possibly unknown individual into your personal space can be daunting or even dangerous. For that reason, I suggest limiting tenant option to people you already know. Once you feel comfortable, this can be a great way to generate income from an otherwise unused space.

If you do not currently own a home and are looking to move, try finding a roommate interested in sharing rent. By splitting a rental you each have an equal stake in the property and can get more for your collective dollar than would be possible otherwise. Just be sure to choose a fiscally responsible partner.

When I bought my first house, it was a 3 bedroom, 2.5 bath, 2 car garage in Flower Mound, Texas. I was a single bachelor at the time but since I always look to the future, I bought with the intention of raising a family some day and therefore wanted the extra space. As it turns out, I ended up having several friends in need of a room to rent. Rather than go out and get their own apartments, I rented 2 rooms at $500 each to them. This effectively cut my bills down to 1/3 of what they would have been otherwise and gave each of them a very cheap and nice alternative to an apartment. We were all saving money each month, living with people we each enjoyed and I was paying off the mortgage on a house at the same time!

Years later after meeting my wife, we ended up deciding to move to another house in a school district more suitable for raising children. Once there, we had another friend willing to rent an upstairs bedroom for $500 per month. Once again we were all saving money each month while living with people we enjoyed.

Interest

I have briefly mentioned it before but let me say an emergency fund is a necessity. I suggest 3 to 6 months of living expenses set aside at all times just in case. By that, I mean enough to cover all of your bills, food, gas and anything else you absolutely cannot cut out. Those funds should remain in an easily accessible, interest bearing account but of course they should be generating as much safe income as possible. That means they should not be in stocks, risky investments or held up for a period of time in a 10 year certificate of deposit (CD). Instead, I suggest an FDIC insured interest bearing account or short term CDs.

Any savings you have beyond the emergency fund can be invested in any way you see fit. A savings account will be the safest and most easily accessible option but will also provide the least amount of interest. A slightly higher interest option is a CD. An interesting trick I learned over the years involves a multiyear CD strategy.

Assume Mr. Rich has $4,000 in a savings account and the highest bang for his buck on CD rates is currently available in a 4 year CD. First, he splits the savings into 4 CDs in the following way.

$1,000 into a 1 year CD

$1,000 into a 2 year CD

$1,000 into a 3 year CD

$1,000 into a 4 year CD

When the first CD matures Mr. Rich reinvests it into a 4 year CD. After 3 years of doing this Mr. Rich will have 1 CD maturing each year while still receiving the higher 4 year interest rate on all of his investments. This can be done with any amount of money, just split it up evenly among the number of years that provides you with the most peace of mind and the largest interest rates.

Whether you choose a savings account, money market account, certificates of deposit or any other investment option, my best suggestion is to shop around. Many banks offer each of these investment options as well as other but some pay much higher interest rates. By shopping around you can be sure to get the highest return on your investment.

6 – Debt, Credit and Interest

According to www.wikipedia.org, "a debt is an obligation owed by one party (the debtor) to a second party, the creditor". A credit is "the granting of a loan and the creation of debt. It is any form of deferred payment". "Interest is a fee paid by a borrower of assets to the owner as a form of compensation for the use of the assets."

The basic concept behind loans, credit cards, cash advances or any other form of credit is that someone has decided to lend you money in order to receive payment with interest in return. When used properly, this can benefit both parties. One receives funds which can be used now to obtain goods or services they could otherwise not afford. The other receives monetary compensation (interest) over the long run for providing the loan.

Unfortunately, many who receive credit either do not understand one of these basic concepts or simply decide the rules must not apply to them. When this occurs, a debt is not repaid which results in either a loss of credit, a reduction in the ability to receive future credit, a repossession of the goods purchased using the credit or all of the above.

A credit rating is the most important factor in obtaining any form of credit. It is a score determined by the three major credit bureaus that rates how responsible you have proven to be with credit in years past and how likely you are to default in the future. Keeping this score high allows you to receive more credit, more easily for less interest because it indicates you are at a low risk for default. The 3 bureaus creditors use to determine your credit score, and therefore your worthiness to receive credit are as follows.

TransUnion (http://www.transunion.com/)

Experian (http://www.experian.com)

Equifax (http://www.equifax.com).

Since you are reading this book, I will assume you understand that any debts accumulated so far must eventually be paid in full. You wish to be a responsible borrower maintaining a high credit rating in order to receive the best possible interest rates. The next few pages will detail how interest and interest rates affect finances. Be warned, math is involved! I promise to try to make it easy to understand though. That being the case, let's start with a simple example of how interest accumulates on a loan over time.

Assume Mr. Rich goes to buy a car that was negotiated down to a price of $20,000. With a high credit rating he is able to qualify for a special 2.9% rate for a 60 month (5 year) loan through the dealership. The resulting monthly payment will be

$358.49. By simply multiplying the monthly payment by the number of months:

$358.49 x 60 Months = **$21,509.40**

We find that at the end of 60 months Mr. Rich will have paid a total of $21,509.40. That equates to $1,509.40 in interest. Not too bad for the privilege of borrowing enough to buy a car.

Now assume Mr. Jones wishes to buy the same car but has a much lower credit rating. With this lower rating he is only able to qualify for a 9.9% interest rate on a 60 month (5 year) loan through the dealership. The monthly payment will now be $423.96, a full $65.47 more than what would have been obtainable with a higher credit score. Multiplying the monthly payment by the number of months results in the following:

$423.96 x 60 Months = **$25,437.60**

At the end of 60 months Mr. Jones will have paid $25,437.60. That equates to $5,437.60 in interest, a full $3,928.20 more than would have been paid with the lower interest rate. As you can see, the single factor of a lower credit score could cost quite a bit!

Regardless of your credit rating and resulting interest rate, I suggest always attempting to either save up for a loan free purchase or to pay loans off early. Take a look at how much interest was paid in the previous examples and compare that to the cost of paying with interest free cash. Without getting a loan at all you would pay $0 in interest saving the entire $1,509.40 or

$5,437.60 to use on other purchases, investments or morning Frappuccinos at Starbucks.

I admit coming up with a lump sum to make large purchases is difficult and not always possible. But fear not, I have tips for everyone! By receiving a loan for a large purchase but paying it off early, you would still pay interest, just less than would be paid if the loan were to go full term. This could easily be done by paying just a bit more each month than the payment requires.

To compare a full term loan versus an early pay off we will use more math. This time we will use a mortgage, as it will provide a better and more obvious example. Assume a $100,000 mortgage with a 6% interest rate over 30 years. The payment would be $599.55 each month for the entire 360 months.

$599.55 x 360 Months = **$215,838**

By taking the full 30 years to pay the loan off you will have paid $215,838 at the end. That's more than double the original amount of the loan!

Now let's assume you think like Mr. Rich and decide to pay an extra $244.31 each month on your 30 year mortgage. That brings your total payment each month up to $843.86. By doing this, the loan will be fully paid off in exactly 15 years rather than 30. Now let's calculate how much will be paid over the 15 years on this loan.

$843.86 x 180 Months = **$151,894.80**

Notice anything interesting? The total amount paid on the loan decreased by almost $64,000! Such a huge savings is possible by simply paying a little more each month. You see, interest is calculated based upon how much money is still owed. By paying the loan down faster, less is owed each month which means less is paid in interest each month. As you can see, over the course of several years this adds up!

Now that the true cost of loans and interest rates is clear, we can move on to credit cards. There are many different cards from many different companies that operate in many different ways. I will focus on those that allow you to make a purchase then pay interest on that purchase while making minimum monthly payments. This seems to include a majority of credit cards available today.

My personal favorite credit card is my Discover Card (www.discovercard.com). This was my very first card that taught all those hard to learn lessons in college. Rather than cut it up after paying it off all those years ago, I kept it as reminder of my victory over debt.

Although I do have several cards, this one is used most frequently for many reasons. First, I can put pretty pictures of Lions and Tigers on the front of the card. I know, it seems like a ridiculous reason to choose a card but I'm saying this to prove a point. How often has something like a pretty package swayed your judgment? Be cautious of that as the best wrapped items are not always what they seem.

So back to my real reasons for preferring this card. After being a cardholder for so many years, Discover has opted to provide a reasonably high limit which enables me to make any purchase I deem necessary. With a high credit score, never missing a payment or going over my limit, Discover has also provided a very low interest rate. Finally, this card offers bonus awards for using it and does not charge an annual fee.

With all of the interest calculations we did for loans earlier, the interest rate on credit cards should come as no surprise. Credit companies are basically offering an on demand loan while asking for some amount of interest in return. The interest rate from one card to another varies widely but is usually higher than any type of fixed term loan. Basically the privilege of getting an instant loan on demand costs more.

The nice thing about a credit card is that interest is not usually charged if the balance is paid in full each month. This effectively turns into a free 1 month loan each month. When used responsibly, this can be a great convenience. Rather than carry large sums of cash or a checkbook around, you can simply carry a single credit card which is used to pay for everything. At the end of the month a single payment is made to the credit card company for all of the expenses incurred.

If you do decide to carry a balance and therefore pay interest, be sure that balance gets paid off as soon as possible. Since credit cards are a high cost of debt due to the high interest rates they charge, this is a very bad long term investment. Each month interest is calculated based upon the outstanding balance. If the card is never paid off and only the minimum monthly payment is sent, it could take many years to eventually pay it off completely. Plus, you will most likely still be using the card and accumulating more debt in the mean time. If you have more than one card, the responsibility is increased as a multi-debt, high interest scenario can quickly kill financial stability.

This is especially true for very high interest cards such as those offered by department stores. How often have you heard a phrase like "Would you like to save 10% today by applying for our store credit card?" Although it sounds like a great idea at first, that card will most likely have a much higher than average interest rate. Not only that, by applying for one card after another, you are increasing the number of inquiries to your credit as each creditor has to check your score before approving an application. This is one of those items the three credit bureaus use to determine your score. More inquiries equal a lower score which ends up translating into higher interest.

Thankfully it is not necessary to cancel all of your credit cards in order to find newer options with lower interest rates. Sometimes simply calling an existing credit card company and asking for a lower interest rate works wonders. If you have a good history with them, they might just lower the rate on the spot. This method has worked well for me in the past.

With all of that in mind, there are a few important points to remember. First, paying the card off each month will allow you to avoid paying any interest at all which is the most desirable situation. Second, a low interest rate is always desirable in the case that a balance needs to be carried from one month to another. Third, too many inquiries will reduce your credit score and therefore increase your interest rate. Fourth, credit cards are debts that will need to be repaid, they are not free money.

By living within your means and spending less than you earn, interest, credit inquiries and compound debt should never be an issue. If all expenses are within the available income each month, paying of all credit cards in full should be easy to do.

Now that you have a basic idea of how credit works and why it can be useful, it is worth noting that my credit card interest rates no longer matter as I never carry a balance. Instead, everything possible is paid for with my Discover Card which is then paid off in full each month. Does this sound odd to you? It might as very few people I know do this. The reason is not only for the extreme convenience, but also because it provides free bonuses. Yes, I said "free bonuses" and will explain that next.

Credit card bonuses can be very lucrative. My wife and I each have a favorite card and each have different but valuable bonus structures. The basic concept for most cards goes something like this. Each time the card is used a percentage of that purchase will be accumulated as some form of bonus points. Once enough points have been accumulated, they can be redeemed for some type of reward.

In my case, Discover Card rewards me each time I make a purchase and updates a dollar amount that I have available for a reward. I can choose to use that reward to pay my bill, increase the reward by spending it at a preferred partner or even use that reward directly on Amazon (www.amazon.com) to pay for a purchase. How often do you get a free convenience that actually pays you to use it? By charging everything I can and paying it off immediately, that is exactly what my credit card offers!

Speaking of bonuses, there are actually a few benefits to department store credit cards. Assuming you do not carry a balance, they can be very lucrative too. My wife and I each have credit cards to our favorite clothing stores that regularly send out coupons as well as allow the accumulation of points which can be uses for free clothing. By combining the coupons, in store sales or clearance racks and these points, we are able to regularly purchase all of our clothing for more than 50% off of retail price. Once again, we are getting paid to use a free convenience they offer!

If you feel confident in your ability to pay off every credit card each month without ever allowing a balance to carry over month to month, I will explain a few of my tricks. Please keep in mind that these only work if you actually pay all cards off every month.

- Ensure the credit card does not have an annual fee. This will cut into the valuable benefits.

- Have all possible bills paid automatically with your favorite credit card each month. Not only will this generate a lot of bonus points each month, it will be more convenient and will save money on stamps.
- Charge groceries, food, gas or anything else you would normally pay cash for to the credit card.
- If you fly frequently, obtain a credit card that ties into frequent flier points for an airline. This will assist in receiving free flights on a regular basis which could be used for a vacation!
- If you shop somewhere regularly, sign up for a store credit card that provides special benefits at that store.

By following these tips and paying off any accumulated debt in full each month, bonuses and convenience are yours for the taking!

7 – Avoid Spending Money

The new favorite American past time appears to be shopping. Think about that for a few minutes. How many places are within 10 minutes of home that would happily allow you to shop till you drop? When boredom sets in and an entertaining escape is desired, what pops into your mind first? For most, the answer is a trip to a local mall, strip mall or shopping center.

While this can definitely be entertaining, it is not going to help your finances or contribute to living within your means. I will provide several entertainment alternatives in a bit, but for now let's confront this shopping obsession head on. Since you are now focused on changing your mindset and spending less than you earn, why not begin before even leaving home. If heading to the store for groceries, go and buy what is needed. Otherwise, start by asking some of the following questions.

"Can I make do for now?"

"Is it possible to make items I currently own last a little longer?"

"Can I fix something that's currently broken rather than buy new?"

"Am I going to shop out of necessity or boredom?"

Once you have decided the trip is actually out of necessity, make a list of the items needed and head to the store. Once at the store remember to mentally separate what you *need* from what you *want*. The list made prior to leaving the house will make this task much easier as you will be less likely to indulge in impulse purchases.

Speaking of impulse purchases, do you ever window shop? How often does window shopping result in the purchase of an item you never thought you needed until it appeared in that window? Assuming you do actually find an item that could improve some aspect of life, rather than buy it immediately let the idea simmer for a week. During that week ask yourself whether that item is really necessary, what benefits it would provide and how life would be without it. If the item is in fact useful, determine how often it will be used and whether it would be beneficial to borrow a similar item from a friend rather than purchase a new one. Doing all of this will help to weed out unnecessary impulse purchases which will in turn reduce expenses.

How often have you made a purchase simply because someone close by bought that item first? Or maybe you heard it was the best thing since sliced bread! Did it look cool and entertaining? Did the friend convince you of the amazingly life changing effects of item *xyz*? Did life actually change after the purchase? If not, is the purchase now a regret? By reflecting on the past it is often possible to avoid making similar mistakes in the future.

A perfect example of this is the popularity of an iPad made by Apple (www.apple.com). It is no secret that Apple has mastered the art of advertising and public relations. They are capable of creating a device, making it popular and convincing everyone that it is a must have before consumers even know how they would use it. So many times I have heard "I want an iPad so bad!" But when asked why, the response is usually something similar to "Because it's cool!" If pressed further and asked what they will use the device for, a common response is "I don't know I'll figure that out after I get one!"

Don't get me wrong, this is an impressive accomplishment by Apple. But from a frugal consumer's perspective, this is a horrible way to buy products. Any large purchases must be considered in depth including a comparison of cost to benefit. If you do not yet know how something will be used (the benefit), it is not actually needed. Something that is desired but not necessary is what we call a luxury item.

Now that it is clear how to avoid large and unnecessary purchases I will let you in on a little secret. No matter how frugal you become, there will always be one or more luxury item you want. These might be a complete waste of money but the desire remains. Eventually everyone succumbs to the desire for a splurge purchase so why not plan for it?

I suggest finding several ways to save up for these items. Having a change jar near the door that loose coins are consistently dropped into is one great method. Small, barely noticeable sums can add up to quite a bit over time. If you have decided to participate in some of the alternative income sources mentioned previously, use those proceeds to fund luxury purchases. If unexpected sums of money come in the form of gifts, tax returns or rebates, try setting those aside for a splurge.

Planning for splurge purchases on luxury items might also result in some unexpected side effects. By not immediately buying something, it may lose its appeal or might even be forgotten about completely. By saving up for the item there will be time to read reviews and verify that it will suit your needs. If it does not, skip the purchase and money will be saved. Most importantly for items you do end up buying, anticipation will build making the final purchase that much more satisfying.

I promised to provide some entertainment alternatives to shopping so let's get started. Of course, these will need to be less expensive alternatives as the goal is financial stability and living within your means. With that said, the best way to start is to list out all of the possible forms of entertainment you are aware of. From there, determine which ones provide the best bang for your buck and how to reduce their costs as much as possible.

Have you ever looked at the cost per hour of various things you enjoy doing for entertainment? Sometimes, what initially appears to be a cheap method of entertainment ends up being fairly expensive when the amount of time it lasts is factored in. For example, the entry fee to a local zoo provides several hours of fun and is a much better value than a one hour trip to a fancy restaurant.

Assuming you already have some basic toys, kicking or throwing a ball is a freebie that could provide an unlimited amount of fun. Take those toys to a local park with some friends for even more entertainment. These activities also provide the added benefit of exercise which is definitely lacking for the average American.

For those looking for something a little more interesting, how about comparing the cost of some common paid away from home activities to similar activities at home? How far will $20 go at an arcade? How about at a movie theater? How many hours of entertainment will you get for that $20? Now think about how many hours $20 could provide in video game or movie rentals to play and watch at home. Also consider how many different used movies or games could be purchased for that same $20. If you enjoy video games, compare the cost of purchasing one new or used game per month to the cost of purchasing a multiplayer online game with a small monthly subscription. Which provides more hours of entertainment for your money? Similarly, compare the monthly subscription cost of a video service like Netflix (www.netflix.com) to buying or renting movies.

My wife and I actually stopped going out to movies years ago. Not only has the cost of entry increased to levels we are not willing to pay, but the cost of snacks has also gone up while quality has gone down. Beyond just cost, we have found that when sharing a movie with several hundred others there is usually someone talking and reducing our overall enjoyment. Add to that the fact that I inevitably need to use the restroom during an action scene and suddenly a movie theater becomes much less attractive. Not only is staying home to watch a movie cheaper, but also more enjoyable.

Now I suggest we review some older entertainment options that I grew up with. When was the last time you played a card or board game? By purchasing a single card or board game each week for around $10 a piece, you are investing in a form of entertainment that can literally last a lifetime. Purchasing a single standard deck of cards can even provide dozens of possible games. A quick search online can provide a wealth of card game options. In addition to being cheap and reusable options, by asking family and friends to play you are will also end up strengthening relationships.

Children and adults alike can enjoy hours of entertainment putting together a jigsaw puzzle, making amazing Lego (www.lego.com) creations, reading a book, solving puzzles or coloring and painting. By purchasing these items once, an endless amount of cheap entertainment can be available for years to come.

For additional savings try to buy these items on sale, using coupons or look for used versions on websites like eBay (www.ebay.com) and Craigslist (www.craigslist.org). Legos, books and board games have a very long lifespan so gently used versions will always provide a welcome discount.

Beyond just cost savings and bonding, some of these items will also encourage imagination. As a child, a cardboard box could become a house, fort or ship. A book could take you to a far away land where anything was possible. Can you say the same now? Can your children?

One last possibility I will leave you to think about is that of community events. Many communities offer public events for little to no cost. Community pools, parades, festivals and fireworks show options are just a few. These allow socialization with those nearby as well as an inexpensive way to have a great time. Once again, you can have fun while building relationships with those around you!

8 – Moderation

While spending less, making more and learning to live as frugally as possible are great, too much of a good thing can quickly turn bad. How often have you started a strict diet in the hopes of losing weight only to crash with a buffet splurge meal? The same can happen with finances if the pressure to save becomes overwhelming. The answer to both is moderation.

Wikipedia (www.wikipedia.org) describes moderation as "the process of eliminating or lessening extremes". Applied to dieting it means not jumping into the most miserable diet you can think of. For finances it means taking everything one step at a time and trying a little bit of each method until a happy medium is found. Imagine eating unflavored beans and rice at every meal in order to spend the least possible amount on groceries. Now imagine sitting in the sweltering heat without air conditioning in order to reduce an electric bill. While both will accomplish the intended goal, neither will be a pleasurable or sustainable solution.

By doing everything in moderation a happy medium or equilibrium can be found that will be sustainable over long periods. Small steps allow a gradual movement and when combined with an overall change in mindset can slowly change an entire lifestyle. But once this new lifestyle has set in, there will still be needs and desires for luxury goods, services or entertainment. Rather than eliminating these items completely it helps to plan for and to integrate them into the new lifestyle.

As you may have noticed, splurge purchases have been mentioned a few times already. They should already be included in the budget created in chapter 4 and alternative methods of saving for splurges were discussed in chapter 7. This was deliberate since they are a necessary part of every lifestyle and therefore should be planned for. The key is to partake of splurges in moderation while also saving, spending less and attempting to make more.

Keep this concept in mind as you continue reading and learning. Try each of the tips provided in small quantities at first, then increase at a rate that feels comfortable. Moderation truly is one of the primary keys to a happy life and living within your means so think of how it could be applied to the lessons presented so far as well as those to come.

9 – Emergency Fund

The focus of this book so far has been to explain the basics of living within your means. By explaining the basics and offering specific ways to spend less and earn more, I hope to have instilled a new confidence in you that can be used each day. The next valuable tool I will go over in detail is savings and more specifically an emergency fund.

All too often I see people nearby living like the Joneses, paycheck to paycheck. Their focus is on how the next bill will get paid rather than saving. The end result is that they barely manage to keep up with things right up until an unexpected event occurs. From an illness to a flat tire, these things do happen and it is up to every individual to be prepared. These situations can be devastating and the added stress of wondering how to pay for them can make matters worse.

An unexpected car breakdown is exactly what caused my debt situation in college. If I had planned ahead, cut costs, increased savings and created an emergency fund, the unexpected expense could have easily been paid for. By doing so, I could have potentially avoided the years of debt that resulted from that single event. Likewise, for those living paycheck to paycheck, a single extra expense could be the difference between making ends meet and a never ending debt spiral.

A commonly suggested emergency fund is 3 to 6 months of living expenses. My suggestion is 6 months of living expenses as it provides a large cushion and more importantly, peace of mind. This amount can help to pay for any unexpected expenses or to pay bills if a job loss occurs. That might seem like a lot of money right now and that is exactly how I used to feel. Saving enough to cover 6 months of bills is not an easy task but with a little effort, persistence and time it can be done.

Assuming the tips provided so far have allowed you to obtain a balance between income and expenses with a bit left over each month, it is time to start building your own emergency fund. The last thing you want to do is run out to find a shiny new toy to buy with the extra money. Ok, that might the first thing you *want* to do but what you *need* to do is save it.

By learning to set aside any extra income, a pool of money will always be available to pull from when needed. Initially the pool will be small but something is better that nothing. In time, the full 6 months of living expenses and more can be accumulated. Anything beyond that base 6 month amount could be used for luxury items, paying down a mortgage or just left alone to gain interest. If you find saving difficult, a tried and true method to ensure extra money is not spent is to set up an automatic transfer from a checking to a savings account. Most banks offer this feature and it helps by removing the thought of that extra money from your mind.

By consistently saving, you will eventually reach your emergency fund goal and the stability it provides. Be patient and diligent and success will be yours. In the end, by planning for the unexpected, hard times can end up feeling a little softer and harder times can hopefully be avoided.

10 – Repurpose, Reuse, Recycle

With many of the basic concepts now well in hand and an emergency fund accumulating, it is time to move towards more creative ways of living within your means. Beyond just making more, spending less and saving, it is possible to learn to thrive with what you already have. Not only does this decrease current expenses, but it also helps to recession proof your finances by providing tools that can be used in times of need.

The first tools I will explain are those of repurposing, reusing, and recycling items you already have. In a previous chapter, I had you ask the following questions before leaving on a shopping trip:

"Can I make due for now?"

"Is it possible to make items I currently own last a little longer?"

"Can I fix something that's currently broken rather than buy new?"

Revisiting those same questions with the intention of repurposing, reusing, and recycling can open a world of possibilities. This could mean renewing the life of an old chair by simply sanding and repainting. Sanding and re-staining multiple pieces of furniture can even result in unmatched pieces becoming matching sets. Reupholstering your favorite recliner not only saves money, it keeps an old friend around a bit longer.

Do you have a dog? Fancy dog beds can be found at any local pet store but an old, worn out comforter works just as well. Rather than throwing out old comforters, sheets, blankets, towels or pillows, give your pets a hand me down gift. If you do not have pets, use these items as shop rags or drop cloths when painting. If you have any sewing skills these items can become curtains, bags, purses or even a patchwork quilt. You could even make eco friendly, recycled shopping bags to help the environment while saving money! Who knew there were so many uses for old cloth items?

A fond memory of mine is building forts using various sized cardboard boxes. Any time a new large appliance was purchased, it was followed by a weekend of imaginative fun. If you have kids, save any cardboard boxes you come across in an attic or storage area. When inexpensive fun is desired, bring a few of them out and hand them to your kids. Make a house, a car, a boat or a castle with just a box, some scissors and tape.

How often do you throw away or recycle food containers? Next time, think of ways you could recycle it. No, I don't mean by throwing it into the recycle bin, but definitely do that if you cannot find another use. I have found that a used up parmesan cheese container works great as a snack container for kids. My daughter loved to shake one filled with cereal as a baby. Not only did it store her snacks, it gave her a great toy too! As a matter of fact, emptied food containers are great for storing pretty much anything you can imagine around the house as well as making entertaining toys or crafts. Try making a homemade candle using some old wax and a tin can for a fun, family bonding experiment.

A great way to save money at the store while also reusing at home is to buy concentrate. Concentrated juices and cleaning supplies are two great examples that cost less at the store than their fully hydrated counterparts. By putting them into previously purchased containers, you save money as well as the environment by not creating additional waste. Next time you are at the store, try a cost comparison of items you use that offer concentrated options and see if this makes sense.

Do you have an attic, shed or basement full of old items? Many families store items when they are no longer needed and end up forgetting about them. Take some time to go through all the boxes and dusty furniture in any storage areas you have to see if they can be reused today. It might be possible to completely redecorate or refurnish a room without leaving the house!

If you ever feel the need to go out and purchase a new technology gadget, definitely take a look around to see if something you already have can be used instead. A brand new iPod Touch (www.apple.com) may not be necessary if you still have an older mp3 player. Is it really necessary to get a new Gazillion Gigabyte model of a music player, video player or laptop if you're only using a fraction of that on the current model? Is a new TV or gaming system really necessary or will yours last a few more years?

Is a new car really necessary? Could $1,000 put into your current car make it last another year? Compare that to the monthly payment and insurance cost on a brand new car. From a purely monetary standpoint, it might be better to stick with what you have. This of course does not apply if your used car is falling apart or hazardous, but it is worth considering.

If you have items around the house you absolutely cannot find a new use for and plan to throw out, give them to a local charity. By doing so, you are not only helping others in your area but also gaining a valuable tax deduction that can be claimed when preparing next year's tax documents.

Hopefully this chapter has provided plenty of food for thought. By using the specific examples I provided and adding a few of your own, it might be possible to reduce consumption and expenses, revive old belongings, help the environment or help out a local charity. All of these are worth the effort.

11 – Coupons, Sales and Discounts

I have yet to find a better way to save money on everyday expenses than by finding coupons, sales or discounts. There are simply too many day to day expenses that cannot be reduced any other way. Although coupon clipping and hunting for good deals sounds tedious and time consuming, it doesn't have to be. By using a few easy methods you can have plenty of options with very little effort.

Discount Cards

We all need to eat and have several common necessities we can't go without so the grocery store is a great place to start. Most stores have some kind of discount card so be sure to sign up for one wherever you shop. They are usually offered by simply filling out a quick form at the checkout register so this is a very quick option. Once you have one, any current sales in the store will be given to you with no additional effort required. In addition to that, many stores offer extra savings based on your purchases as long as you always scan that card.

A major grocery chain in my area offers discounted gas every so often if you have spent a certain amount at their store. Another chain I used a few years back offered me a free turkey at Thanksgiving for spending a certain amount at that store while scanning my card. In both cases I have received free items and discounts by simply doing normal, weekly shopping. I can't help but get excited about freebies that require no extra effort!

Coupons

Many stores beyond just grocers offer email distribution lists you can sign up for that will result in coupons and upcoming sale information being sent to your inbox weekly. My wife and I are both signed up to receive email offers from all of the stores we shop at most frequently. By simply checking our email, we are always up to date on the best prices for the items we find interesting. As mentioned previously in this book, email coupons in combination with other specials from a store credit card allow us to purchase all of our clothing for 50% off or more. Once again, with very little effort we are able to save quite a bit with each purchase.

Take some time to think about all of the stores you shop at regularly. Add to that all of the restaurants you typically eat at. Now think about all of the online retailers you have used in the past year. How many companies on your list have websites? Try visiting the website for each of those retailers and see if they offer an option to sign up for a discount mailing list. You may be surprised to find that even small restaurants and stores offer up email discounts on a regular basis. A local family owned, single store Italian restaurant I visit sends buy one entree, get one half off coupons to my email address every few weeks. One near you may too, but you won't know until you look.

Now that taking advantage of the easy discounts has been discussed, let's talk coupons. There are so many ways to find coupons these days. Many people have forgotten that Sunday newspapers are still packed full of them. Try picking one up the next time you are out on a weekend and see how much money it saves you. I'm sure you can find more than enough savings to warrant the cost of the paper.

Do you receive frequent junk mail? Does it normally go straight into the trash or recycle bin? Next time try actually reading through it all to look for offers of interest. I often find several valuable coupons hidden in junk mail that would have been thrown away had I not taken the time to look. Several times catalogues were placed in the recycle bin upside down revealing a coupon on the back for a percentage off of my next purchase. If I don't plan to purchase by the expiration date, I let the coupon go. But if there is any chance a need to shop at that store may arise, the coupon gets clipped and saved.

Beyond providing discounts on everyday items you need, coupons found from any of the previously mentioned sources can often provide an opportunity to try out a retailer or product that is new to you. If Friday night comes along and you are in the mood to go out to eat, try going to one of the places for which you now have a coupon. If it is for a place you are familiar with, the result is a discounted meal at a place you love. Otherwise, it could be a great opportunity to try something new.

If in need of a household cleaning product or food item from the store and you have a coupon for a different brand, try it. You may find the new, discounted item to be better than the brand normally bought. If not, at least it was an opportunity to try something for less than the normal price.

There are a few additional coupon sources online to explore that can provide valuable discounts. Groupon (www.groupon.com) is one that has been growing in popularity recently. This online coupon giant works with local retailers to provide them business while also providing discounts to the local population. By signing up for their mailing list, frequent deals to retailers you may already be using will be provided on a regular basis. By going to the Groupon website frequently many other discounts are also available.

A quick search in your favorite online search engine for "online coupons" will bring back a variety of additional options. These change frequently but I have been able to find many sites that allow for printing of coupons for anything you can imagine. One example used recently is www.coupons.com which provides current coupons for a wide variety of products. From groceries, to clothing, restaurant to oil changes or car washes, many options are available with just a few clicks of the mouse.

Another online example that also sends coupons to my physical mail box is Valpak (www.valpak.com). They specialize in coupons for retailers in many local areas. By entering your city or zip code on their website, coupons to business nearby are presented and sorted by category. As you can see, all it takes is a few minutes on the internet with a purpose to find a wealth of coupons and discounts.

Promotion Codes

Online retailers frequently have a little box on their order entry screens labeled something like "promotion code". This is basically a coupon that requires the entry of a code that was typically provided via email. Sometimes this code is provided as a result of a previous order, sometimes from discount email lists you have signed up for. Regardless of where the discount comes from, it will always mean less money out of your pocket which is great!

Thankfully, there are some websites out there that collect these promotion codes and post them for anyone to use. My favorite is Retail Me Not (www.retailmenot.com) as they usually have the largest number of reliable coupon codes that will work when an attempt is made to use them. By simply going to their website and typing your favorite store into the search box, you can choose from a list of current coupons that may fit your needs.

The great thing about online promotion codes is that you don't need to clip coupons or do any planning ahead of time.

Simply look for a promotion code box on the checkout page of any online purchase you intend to make. If you find one, do a quick search on your favorite search engine or promotion code website to see if a promotion is available that could save you money.

I can't count the number of times I have been in mid purchase and decided to do a quick search for a promotion code that has resulted in a discount. Sometime a code is found for free shipping, other times there might be one for a percentage off of the entire order. In either case, money was saved with minimal effort which is the important lesson to be learned.

Sales

When you walk into a store, where do you head first? Is it straight to the items written down on a list previously? Is it to something flashy in the store window? How about to items currently on display near the entryway? Usually items in the window or on a special display are simply those items the store wants you to buy for the current season. This also usually means these items are full price and very profitable for the retailer.

All too often I see friends of mine fall for this marketing technique. Rather than look for sales or discounts, they head straight to whatever caught their eye first. The end result is a very expensive trip with only a few items to show for it. Next time you go shopping, try heading straight to the clearance rack instead. This is especially true for clothing stores as the clearance rack holds a wealth of options.

At my favorite clothing retailer, I usually arrive with coupons in hand and head straight to the clearance rack. After going through everything in my size, I select those items that fit the best and only then decide what else may be needed. By doing so, I start with the cheapest possible options in the store and work my way up. To demonstrate the savings potential with this method, let's look at two different people and their experiences shopping for clothes.

Mr. Jones heads to his favorite clothing retailer to buy some new clothes for the current season. He has not put any thought into the trip and therefore does not have any coupons or specific plans. As he walks to the entry way, an impressive display of the current season's styles catch his eye. After entering the store, an additional display of a unique style for this season also attracts his attention.

Each item in the original display Mr. Jones noticed is $50. Each item in the unique style area is $60. Mr. Jones decides to buy 3 items from each display bringing his total purchase to $330. This gives him 6 total items, 3 of which are unique to this season, this year and might look odd if worn next year. Can you think of a style from your past that lasted only 1 season or 1 year? How about bell bottom pants, man Capri pants, pre-torn jeans or skinny jeans? Bell bottoms were revived as flare leg pants several generations later which also died in popularity soon after. Capri pants for men simply never caught on (I wonder why?). The others are still semi-popular but demand is quickly diminishing.

At the same time, Mr. Rich arrives at the same store with a coupon for 20% off of the entire purchase. Ignoring the window displays, Mr. Rich heads straight for the clearance rack. After searching through all of the items in his size, he finds 10 items priced at $10 each that he likes. Some of them are common types of clothing from last season (long sleeve button ups even though spring approaches) that he will be able to wear next year.

From there, Mr. Rich heads to a sale on t-shirts of 2 for $15. He grabs 10 of them and then heads to a sale on jeans and shorts for $25 each. After finding 3 pairs of jeans and 2 pairs of shorts, he heads to the checkout counter. With a total of 25 items his bill adds up to $300. After applying his 20% off coupon, this bill decreases to $240.

Two very different people, with obvious differences in shopping methods ended up with drastically different results. Mr. Jones spent $330 for only 6 items, some of which will be out of style soon. Mr. Rich spent only $240 but managed to head home with 25 items! This is the kind of difference you can expect by using the same judgment as Mr. Rich when shopping. This is also exactly how I shop for my clothes whenever I need them.

Clearance racks are not just for clothing but rather can be found at a wide variety of stores. Next time you are at any store with a clearance rack, take a look. Keep an open mind as well. By purchasing cheap toys on clearance, then hiding them for a few months, you can drastically reduce the cost of birthday or holiday gifts. By purchasing items you know will be useful within the next year, you avoid paying full price when the need for that item arises. Obviously planning ahead with an appropriate set of priorities can make a huge difference.

Loyalty Programs

Quite a few large companies offer loyalty programs. Airlines, hotels, car rentals, cruise ships and restaurants all offer them. Once signed up, points accumulate each time any of the services at these companies are used which can be redeemed later for benefits. Sometimes these programs can also result in email coupons or freebies on your next purchase.

My local hair salon offers a punch card that gets punched each time I get a haircut. After a certain number of visits, a free haircut is provided without having to do anything extra. The sandwich shop next door to the hair salon has the same deal. After so many trips, a free sandwich is available simply for being loyal to that shop. The only thing required in these two cases is remembering to bring the punch card. These are free items provided for simply doing what I normally do. How great is that?

My wife and I have been on a few cruises together in the past and after the first one decided to sign up for their free loyalty program. Since doing that email discounts regularly arrive encouraging us to cruise again. If a nice enough deal is offered at a time we wish to go, the opportunity is seriously considered. In addition to deals for future reservations, this particular program also offers free and discounted drinks as well as special member only activities while on the ship. All of this is available by simply being members of the free club.

If you travel often for work, enrolling in airline, hotel and car rental loyalty programs are a must. Typically, employers do not require or track loyalty programs that their employees use. This allows employees to gain valuable rewards points while travelling on business. In time, these points can add up to free flights, free hotels and free car rentals which can be used for personal vacations. Just think of it as an added perk unintentionally provided by your job.

Speaking of company perks, does your employer offer any discounts to preferred vendors they have special relationships with? If so, look into those deals and use them as often as possible.

Regardless of where discounts are found, always be on the lookout. Sales, clearance racks, internet, newspapers, loyalty programs and your very own mail box can all be great sources of money saving opportunities that you might not currently be using. By taking advantage of all of these together, more can be acquired and while less is spent resulting in rewards and savings you never thought possible.

12 – Cut Future Costs

Have you ever taken time to consider the long term consequences of decisions you make? By reading this book you are obviously interested in taking actions now in order prepare for a brighter financial future. With that step taken and all of the knowledge provided so far you should have a firm grasp on the steps needed to achieve your goals. But there are still many other aspects of life with less obvious long term effects in need of attention.

Health Hazards

Do you smoke? Do you know someone who does? Consider the immediate cost of smoking for a minute. Let's assume our friend Mr. Jones smokes a pack of cigarettes per day at a cost of $5 per pack. That adds up to $1,825 per year or approximately $152 per month. How many other alternatives can you think of that could be purchased for that $152 per month instead?

When creating a budget and cutting items out in order to live within his means, Mr. Rich decided he would rather have cable TV and high speed internet for his $152. The left over money then goes into a savings account to help grow an emergency fund. So he avoids cigarettes completely and spends his hard earned money on items that will entertain and help now while also preparing for the future. Which spending plan makes more sense to you?

Now that we have considered the current cost of smoking how about the long term cost? Smoking has been tied to lung cancer and warns buyers of cigarettes of that fact right on the package. Assuming Mr. Jones gets cancer from smoking, we can imagine the medical costs and lifestyle consequences associated with trying to remove it. Even if cancer is avoided, lung capacity will deteriorate which will make all strenuous activities more difficult. While not a financial cost, this quality of living cost must be taken into account.

Do you exercise? Are you overweight? Just like smoking, being overweight and not exercising have long term consequences on health. High blood pressure, heart attacks, diabetes and strokes are some of the more serious issues that could be faced in the future by maintaining unhealthy habits. Hospital bills, doctor bills, and medicine related to any of these can add up to quite a bit. Less serious issues such as lack of energy, inability to participate in strenuous activities and a poor body image can still drastically affect quality of life.

Any expensive habits that affect health can result in some of the issues mentioned. They drain finances, increase the frequency of doctor visits, increase the chances of medication being required and decrease the overall quality of life. On top of all of that, the opposite (being healthy and in shape) can energize both your body and mind. By thinking more clearly, you will have more brain power to focus on increasing financial stability!

Whether you are more concerned with current finances, future financial stability or health, all of these factors play an important role in preparing for a happy, stable life. I highly encourage avoiding any expensive habits that have been proven as detrimental to your health and to instead get outside for some exhilarating activities. Not only will your wallet thank you, your body and mind will too.

Toys

Do you envy your neighbors because of all of their toys? Do you long for expensive thinks like a Harley (www.harley-davidson.com), a boat or an ATV? Have you ever considered the cost of owning some of those items beyond just the purchase price? I previously touched on this topic, but it is worth reviewing in more detail.

Boats and other recreational vehicles are great examples of how depreciation works. We're all familiar with the old saying that cars lose 10% of their value by just driving them off of the lot. I'm sure that is just an arbitrary number but it is a fact that a car could not be driven off the lot and then resold for the same amount it was bought for. Many products lose value the longer they are owned and this is referred to as depreciation. Recreational vehicles in particular lose value and depreciate very quickly.

A few years back I decided to buy a used Sea Doo Challenger jet boat (www.sea-doo.com). Knowing that new boats cost about the same as a car, depreciate quickly and are typically only used in summer months, I opted to buy used. Since this was something I had wanted for quite a while, I saved up over time and once ready, headed to a local used boat dealer. By finding and purchasing a 4 year old model, I was able to get one for half of the price of a new model along with a few extras. Think about that for a minute. I bought a boat that depreciated 50% of the original purchase price after just 4 years.

For the sake of easy math, let's assume this boat was $20,000 new and that I bought it for $10,000. A loss of $10,000 in value over 4 years is $2,500 per year. If you have been anxiously looking forward to the purchase of a new item like this, be sure to take these numbers into consideration. Knowing you could lose around $2,500 per year definitely changes how attractive a purchase like this appears.

This can be applied to jet skis, motor homes, campers, 4 wheelers, motorcycles, scooters and any other kind of recreational vehicle you can imagine. The rate of depreciation varies by brand and type of product but it always exists. Because of this, any large purchase in this category must be well thought out ahead of time with all costs considered.

If you are not into recreational vehicles, another common recreational toy is a pool. Pools typically increase the value of a home by less than they cost to build and they require quite a bit of maintenance. Chlorine, underwater sweepers, skimmers and filters are just a few of the maintenance items with an associated ongoing cost. Add to that the time it takes to keep the pool cleaned and the allure quickly diminishes.

I know these facts can make many recreational items sound negative but that is not the intention. While some items can be more expensive to own or require more maintenance than others, they might still be exactly what you want or serve a specific need in certain situations. The moral to this story is, consider the future loss of value and maintenance costs for any large purchase up front as those costs affect finances greatly in the long term. If the cost is acceptable, continue with the purchase confident in your decision.

Now that the cost of depreciation is well in hand, consider the cost of maintenance and storage of these toys. Each year I must winterize my boat in order to ensure it runs properly the next year. This typically costs $150 or so but thankfully avoids much larger expenses associated with an engine that stops working. Since it sits for long periods of time, some kind of shelter must be used to protect it. This could be a garage, carport, boat cover or even a rented space in a recreational vehicle storage facility. A cold winter could mean a new battery is needed in the spring. Bringing the battery home to put on a trickle charger requires the purchase of a trickle charger.

The same goes for all recreational vehicles. Motorcycles are typically not ridden in the winter. Off road vehicles are typically only used occasionally when taken to remote locations. Campers are usually only used on weekends or vacations while camping. All of them have different maintenance and storage needs. All of them have batteries and other parts that will deteriorate if not properly maintained.

Do you have expensive china or silverware made from actual silver? How often do you use them? How much did they cost? When my wife and I got married, we knew that china and silver would be on our registry list because we would most likely never find the funds to buy them in the future. Over time we have actually found these items to be of little value to us. The thought of breaking a piece of china prevents regular use, small children compound that fear and life is typically too busy to allow fancy meal creation.

If you have actual silver you already know how much of a hassle that can be. The tarnish that develops can be unsightly and the knowledge that cleaning and polishing will need to occur probably deters use. Have you found owning silver items to be worthwhile? My wife and I opted for fancy looking stainless steel utensils instead which require no maintenance and were a fraction of the cost.

I understand that the luxury items mentioned in this chapter are not obtainable by everyone. But those who cannot afford them often desire them the most. By explaining the cost of ownership, the hope is to temper your desire a bit by providing facts that might not have considered otherwise.

While I do love toys and luxury items as much as anyone, I always consider the cost of ownership before the purchase of a new toy and encourage you to do the same. Not only can the costs add up but the added stress of knowing they must be maintained takes a physical and mental toll as well.

Storage

When redecorating a home, swapping out furniture or buying anything that requires the removal of something else, what happens to the old items? If the answer is that you throw them out or give them away, you could be wasting something that will save money in the future.

A perfectly good dresser that is no longer needed could be thrown out or it could be placed into an attic or storage area to be used by children in years to come. A gently used chair that no longer has a set to match to could be refinished to match a new set in another room. A rug that no longer matches the décor in a room, could very well match the next time redecoration occurs.

I am definitely not encouraging you to become a pack rat or hoarder. But by giving each item some thought, money may be saved in the future. With a selection of gently used items in closets or attic storage, many additional purchases can be avoided by simply scavenger hunting through what you already have. Not only can this be fun, but items with sentimental value can be saved and money conserved in the process.

13 – Home

Home ownership is a big part of the American dream. While apartment living can be very convenient and cost effective, many people aspire to own their own piece of property. With this purchase comes a great deal of responsibility as well as quite a few expenses. In fact, a house is probably the biggest single purchase you will ever make! Thankfully there are many ways to reduce the cost of home ownership which will be discussed in detail in this chapter.

Finding a Home

A good place to begin is with the initial search for a home. While building a brand new mansion in the fanciest gated community around sounds nice, it comes at a very high cost. Instead, look for an area that is located near things that are important to you. If golfing is not something that interests you, that golf course community with premium prices probably is not the best place to start. Also, consider how far away from work the home will be. With gas prices rising, a long commute would add a considerable cost to the new home.

Once a desirable area has been found, spend some time researching the area and watching homes for sale. Get a good idea of what prices are like, what is considered a good deal and which neighborhoods seem to sell most frequently. Every bit of information gathered in this process can reveal important tips that will sway a buying decision. If a neighborhood always has several homes for sale, it could be a good place to find a deal or a place with an undesirable feature that causes everyone to leave. Be sure to learn everything possible before making your first offer.

Now that an area has been located and all of its hidden details are clear, it's time to look for just the right property to buy. Since a house is a large and very expensive purchase that may or may not be easy to sell make sure the purchase is for the long term. When renting, a move is simply a matter of giving notice and finding a new location. When buying, moving requires finding a buyer and paying a series of fairly large fees. Realtor fees alone for selling a home are typically 6% of the sales price so be sure this decision is right for you.

Start by creating a list of all the features a house must have in order to suit your needs for the next 10 years. The following questions are a good place to start. Answers to these and more will help to narrow your search for the perfect home.

- How many bedrooms are needed right now?
- Do you plan to start or expand a family?

- How many bedrooms will be needed 5 years from now?
- How many bathrooms will be needed to support everyone that will be living there?
- Is a yard important?
- Is a pool important?
- Are views out of windows important?
- Is the direction the house faces important? In hotter states a West facing back yard is like an oven in summer months.
- How large does the house need to be in order to support your lifestyle?

With a great idea of the location and features needed, it's time to find the house worthy of an offer. Calling a realtor and searching through the current MLS listings is a very common way to look. Websites such as www.realtor.com are a great place to view MLS listings from home at your convenience. Driving around the area of interest looking for sale signs can also be a great method of searching.

The listing price of a house is determined by the seller. Some people assume their property should be worth more and therefore price it higher. Others have already moved and therefore price the property lower in order to sell quickly. Sometimes the seller isn't an individual at all. It could be a bank that recently foreclosed and now wants to sell to recoup their loan funds. These factors and more go in to the asking price and must be taken into consideration in order to find the best deal.

Foreclosures, short sales, fixer uppers, buyers who need to sell soon and properties that have been on the market for a while will all be priced lower than others in the area. Be sure to have a realtor look for these factors, as great deals can sometimes be found on houses in these situations. Once that option has been exhausted, look for homes already priced reasonably. Sometimes good deals can be found while other times the search simply results in low priced money pits requiring time and effort to repair. A reputable inspection service can help to ensure you avoid homes with issues.

Purchasing a Home

During the house hunt, be prepared to jump on a great deal once it has been found. Start by getting prequalified for a home loan. Shop around to find a lender with good rates then start the prequalification process there. It is always possible to switch to a different lender later if necessary so the prequalification itself should be the area of focus. This not only tells the seller you are a capable buyer, it also allows you to understand how much a bank will be willing to lend.

When picking a lender the most important things to look for are the interest rate, points and fees. The rate will determine what percentage of the loan you will pay in interest each year. Points are an upfront cost paid in order to obtain a lower overall interest rate. While more expensive in the beginning, they result in a lower loan payment which will save you money in the long run. What this means is that paying extra points may not be worthwhile if you plan to live in the house only a few years. Be sure to review your point and interest rate options in detail with a mortgage broker. Loan fees can vary widely in cost and type so be sure to get those specified up front to ensure no hidden costs appear later.

It is worth noting that the specific details of a loan can greatly affect the value. Hidden caveats such as a prepayment penalty, balloon payment at the end or a variable interest rate after a short fixed rate period could spell disaster for finances. Since those can vary greatly, the assumptions provided here will be based on a standard fixed rate loan without any caveats.

Once you have picked the lender, been prequalified for a mortgage and found the perfect house, it's time to make an offer! I will leave the details of this to you and a real estate professional. Assuming the area has been researched and the perfect property found in an ideal location for a great price, you are in great shape. All of the steps provided so far have been meant to help save as much money as possible while ensuring the future value of your investment.

Now that an offer has been made and a contract on a house has been signed, it's time to follow through with a loan while once again saving as much money as possible. There are many options to choose from but I suggest sticking with a standard fixed rate mortgage. The 2 most common fixed rate mortgages to choose from are 15 year and 30 year. The primary differences are the length of time and the interest rate. Shorter loans offer lower rates than longer loans so the rates on 15 year loans should always be less than the rates on the 30 year loans. The decision on the length of this mortgage is a big one. In order to show the difference, check out the following example.

Assume the new house is being sold for $200,000 and you are putting 20% down on a fixed rate mortgage. Also assume the 30 year mortgage rate will be 6% while the 15 year rate will be 5%. The following calculations show the monthly cost difference.

$160,000 @ 6% for 30 years = **$959.28/month**

$160,000 @ 5% for 15 years = **$1265.27/month**

At first glance, it is obvious that the 30 year loan costs less each month. But what is not obvious is how much interest and principal are included in those payments. So to get a better idea of the overall cost of each loan, let's multiply the payments out over the life of each of the loans.

$959.28/month * 12 months * 30 years = **$345,340.80**

$1265.27/month * 12 months * 15 years = **$227,748.60**

Is that what you expected? Which do you think Mr. Rich would opt for? Which do you think the Joneses would have chosen? By paying the higher mortgage payment each month on the 15 year loan with a lower interest rate, you would save $117,592.20 over the life of the loan. Suddenly the 30 year mortgage doesn't look all that great! If at all possible, I suggest opting for a 15 year mortgage when financing a house. If that is not an option, the next best solution is to get a 30 year mortgage but pay a little extra each month in order to pay the loan off sooner and end up paying less in interest.

Assume you get the same 30 year mortgage from above, but follow Mr. Rich's method and put an extra $100 per month towards it. This will give you the option to pay less on months where money is tight and then make up for it when more is available. By paying an extra $100 each month, the entire loan will be paid off in approximately 23.5 years. The following calculations will show the resulting cost difference.

$959.28 + $100 /mo * 12 months * 23.5 yrs = **$298,716.96**

$345,340.80 original - $298,716.96 = **$46,623.84 savings**

By paying an extra $100 per month towards the 30 year loan, you will save over $46,000 in interest over the life of the loan and pay it off 6.5 years early! I highly suggest finding an online mortgage calculator and playing with the numbers from the previous example to see how paying extra affects each situation. Then by taking this information and applying it to your own unique situation in the future, plenty of money can be saved and headaches avoided. This will increase financial stability now and in the future.

Refinance

Sometimes rates fall making a refinance loan attractive. The basic concept is that a lender pays off an existing mortgage and issues a new one. In the process, fees are paid to the lender and hopefully a lower interest rate is obtained. The only piece of advice I can provide here is to be sure to accurately calculate how long it will take for the lower interest savings to offset the cost of the refinance fees. If the refinance costs would take 5 years to pay back but you plan on moving in 3 years, stick with the existing mortgage even if the rate is higher.

Moving

If you happen to move locally and have the option to use a single realtor to sell one house and buy another, be sure to ask for a discount on agent fees. Many agents will be happy to provide a combined service discount for using them multiple times if you just ask. At the same time, be wary of real estate firms that offer to sell a home for a reduced 3% rate rather than the standard 6% rate. The fee is typically split as 3% to the seller's agent and 3% to the buyer's agent. Agents representing buyers will want a full 3% fee for themselves regardless of what the seller's firm states. With that in mind, buyer's agents might avoid showing a property to their clients if their profit is going to be less than normal. This is not to say that reduced fee real estate firms are bad, there are just some side effects to take into consideration when using them.

Deductions

One of the benefits of having a mortgage is that the government allows a write off on any taxes and interest paid on that loan. If you currently itemize deductions, payments on a mortgage can make a big difference. If you do not currently itemize, ask an accountant whether it would be beneficial to your specific circumstances. The end result is more cash back when taxes are filed each year.

Home Repair

Now that the home is yours, think about ways to save money on any ongoing home repairs and improvements. Many home projects can be done by anyone with a bit of carpentry, plumbing or general handyman skills.

Painting is a cheap and easy do it yourself weekend task and can make a great difference in a house. Walls, ceilings, trim and furniture are all great candidates for a quick coat of paint. Leaky faucets, backed up toilets, fences or deck staining are all great little home improvement projects for the weekend do it yourselfer. With a little knowledge and possibly some help from a friend, plenty of money can be saved by tackling these tasks yourself.

While some projects are easily done by anyone, others are better left to professionals. Often times well meaning homeowners will attempt to save money by doing work themselves only to create a disaster in the process. The result could cost more to fix than hiring a professional would have been in the first place. Keep this in mind when projects are selected and only attempt those you are confident in your ability to complete. Remember, the goal is to cut costs and save money.

14 – Energy Efficiency

Whether in a house, apartment or other type of home, electricity will be prevalent all around you. It is used to run everything from a coffee maker to a computer to air conditioning that makes a room comfortable and of course with these conveniences comes a cost. In recent years the news has been filled with articles on rising energy costs, viability of alternative fuels and of course, energy efficiency.

The idea behind energy efficiency is nothing more than attempting to use less energy to maintain the same quality of life. There are many way to do this including turning things off when not in use or opting to buy an appliance that has been manufactured to consume less energy than its predecessor. Over the next few pages I will describe a few tips picked up over the years from personal experiences.

Many times energy consuming items at home use power simply because they are left on when not in use. Turn off lights, the TV or other electronics in rooms when no one is using them. This might not make a huge difference depending on current habits, but if your house is typically lit up like an airport runway day and night this would be an easy way to reduce utility bills.

Central air conditioning and heating have always been the prime consumers of energy in my home. Thankfully there are few very easy ways to decrease this consumption. Start with a programmable thermostat to set the temperature lower or higher when you aren't home (warmer in summer, colder in winter). When no one is home, the change in temperature will not be noticed but the energy savings will. In summer try setting the temperature 1 degree higher while everyone is home and offsetting the difference with a fan. Fans use much less energy than central AC and can be targeted directly where needed rather than cooling the entire house. In winter try decreasing the thermostat temperature and offsetting the difference with extra clothing or a blanket.

While heating and cooling are the largest expenses in my home, there are several methods of reducing the need for those conveniences beyond just using fans and blankets. In hot areas, solar screens, blinds and curtains are a cheap and cost effective method of preventing heat from entering a house. Planting a tree to shade a sunny side of the house can have a similar effect. In older homes, air leaks can allow hot or cold inside air to escape outside. Sealing these leaks can keep temperatures more consistent. A deep layer of insulation will also maintain indoor temperatures by reducing the transfer of heat through the walls and ceiling. These all reduce the need for air conditioning which in turn reduces energy costs.

Speaking of the need for air conditioning, one of the benefits of those systems is that they contain filters to remove particles from the air. While this is a great benefit for removing things like dog hair and allergy causing dust, many people forget to change the filters. An old, clogged filter adds more strain to a central air conditioning system which makes the fan work harder, uses more energy and prematurely wears the system out. Simply replacing the filter every few months can not only reduce energy costs but more importantly can extend the life of the system overall. Keeping something running a few more years obviously saves money and should be done wherever possible.

As time goes on, great strides are made in technology to reduce energy consumption over what previous incarnations of items used. Energy star rated appliances and compact fluorescent light bulbs are great places to start. Both use much less energy than their predecessors and can therefore save money. Be warned though that it is not always cost effective to replace an item with a newer version just to save on energy costs. If a new item costs $100 but will only save $5 over the course of a year and the existing item still works, the purchase is not a wise one.

A less common but very effective way to save money in this area is to look for rebates on energy efficient items. Rebates can be offered from the federal, state or local government or even from a local utility company. The federal government regularly passes bills that offer rebates on things like solar power, high efficiency appliances and insulation. My local utility offers a rebate on AC maintenance services, which ends up offsetting the cost completely. This free service extends the life of my systems at no cost. Keeping an eye out for options such as these can encourage an efficient upgrade or at least offset the cost of one already planned.

15 – Car

Cars can be a source of many financial hurdles. Since loans, interest and comparisons of financing versus paying cash have already been covered in prior chapters, I will skip that topic when it comes to cars. However please keep in mind that the same concepts apply and must be taken into consideration. Also remember to weigh new versus used when making an auto purchase as depreciation applies to cars just as it does to all types of recreational vehicles.

With gas prices rising, news outlets and auto manufacturers have been placing emphasis on improved mileage in recent years. Standard gasoline powered cars are becoming more efficient, alternative energy cars more prevalent and hybrid or all electric cars have planted themselves firmly in the current market.

When looking at these options, be sure to start with the most obvious question. Is a new car necessary? Cars built these days typically last longer than the lemons of long ago, easily lasting 10 or more years without a major break down. There is always a point at which a car will require more repairs than it is worth and anything beyond that time would obviously be a candidate for replacement. Prior to that, be sure to compare the cost of repair to the cost of replacement.

Purchase

Let's review the differences in length of ownership and the cost various options might incur. To start, a comparison of a standard purchase to a new concept called a lease is in order. A lease is effectively a long term rental of an automobile that ends with 2 options.

1. Return the car to a dealership at the end of the lease period and walk away. This works assuming the terms of the lease have been followed and the car has been driven under an agreed upon number of miles.
2. Refinance or pay outright a balloon payment that is supposed to be the remaining value of the car. In this case you keep the car and either pay it off or continue making payments under the refinance terms.

With the concept of a lease understood, it is time to compare how Mr. Rich buys a car to the option Mr. Jones would most likely choose.

The Joneses love shiny new things so when looking for a car they opt for a lease on a beautiful new one. The terms of the lease are as follows.

- They will receive a brand new $35,000 car.
- The lease will run for 2 years.
- The car may be driven up to 12,000 miles per year for a total of 24,000 miles at the end.
- The payment will be $614 per month.
- The residual value of the car will be $26,000 which can either be refinanced or paid outright at the end of the 2 year lease.
- At the end of the lease the dealership will own the car.

Over the course of 2 years, Mr. Jones will own a brand new car that remains in warranty for a total cost of $14,736 or $7,368 per year. At the end of the lease the car will be returned to the dealership and Mr. Jones will move to a new lease on a new car again. Assuming he does this 5 times in a row, ignoring inflation or other complicating factors, over the course of 10 years leasing a car will cost:

$7,368/year * 10 years = **$73,680**

Mr. Rich decides to purchase the same make and model car but using a standard fixed rate loan rather than a lease. He gets a fixed rate 5 year loan and keeps the car for 10 years. With his great credit rating, he qualifies for the lowest possible percentage rate. The terms are as follows:

- The purchase price will be $35,000.
- The annual percentage rate will be 3.9%.
- The loan will be for a 5 year term.
- The car will be kept for a total of 10 years.
- The payment will be $643 per month.
- At the end of the loan period Mr. Rich will own the car.

Using the below calculation we can see how much Mr. Rich will spend on his car:

$643/month * 12 months * 5 years = **$38,580**

After the initial 5 year term, the car will be paid off and Mr. Rich can keep it indefinitely. Assuming he keeps it for another 5 years, after owning the car for a total of 10 years, Mr. Rich will have spent $38,580. Assuming he continues to hold on to the car after 10 years the cost savings increase substantially. Comparing Mr. Rich's choice to Mr. Jones's we see the following end result.

$73,680- $38,580 = **$35,100**

Is that what you expected? By purchasing a used car and holding on to it, Mr. Rich was able to save $35,100 more than Mr. Jones. That's enough to buy a second car! While these calculations are obviously simplified by not including increased maintenance costs or inflation, the core concept should make sense. By opting for the cheapest form of financing and holding onto an item for its entire lifespan, a large sum of money can be available for investment, savings or other purchases.

Let's assume for a minute that Mr. Rich did not purchase a new car but instead bought the same make and model used and 2 years old. This would be the equivalent of Mr. Jones's car at the end of his lease. He gets the same fixed rate 5 year loan and keeps the car for 8 years so the end result is still a 10 year old car at the end. The terms in this case would be as follows:

- The purchase price will be $26,000.
- The annual percentage rate will be 3.9%.
- The loan will be for a 5 year term.
- The car will be kept for a total of 8 years.
- The payment will be $478 per month.
- At the end of the loan period Mr. Rich will own the car.

Using the calculation below we can see how much Mr. Rich will spend on his car:

$478/month * 12 months * 5 years = **$28,680**

Once again, after the initial 5 year term, the car will be paid off and Mr. Rich can keep it indefinitely. Assuming he keeps it for another 3 years, after owning the car for a total of 8 years, Mr. Rich will have spent only $28,680. Just like with buying new, the car could be kept longer if it was taken care of which would result in a substantial increase in cost savings. Just out of curiosity, let's compare the total cost of this used car to what Mr. Jones would do over 8 years.

$7,368/year * 8 years = **$58,944**

$58,944 - $28,680 = $30,264

Once again, the savings would be enough to buy a second car! Try taking some of the concepts learned from earlier chapters and applying them here. How would things change if Mr. Rich paid extra on the loan each month? How would it look if he kept the car longer? There are many choices to be made, each one suited best to a specific situation. Which is best for you?

Now back to the question of whether a car is needed. What if the car you currently own could last another few years? In that case the previous calculations could be postponed while you continue to make use of an item already in your possession. If your family has more than one car, do you actually need all of them? Reducing the number of cars your household has will reduce insurance premiums and overall maintenance costs.

When pondering the question of whether one or more cars are needed, think about alternative forms of transportation. A car is fairly large and can support transporting multiple people and cargo for long distances. Viable alternatives could be a scooter, motorcycle or even just a bicycle. Bicycles provide the added benefit of improving your health on top of being very inexpensive but typically only transport a single person without cargo. If you live in an area with a dense population there may also be public forms of transportation available for a small cost. Busses and trains are very common, cheap and efficient methods of getting to a destination in many cities across the country.

Regardless of what your specific needs are, understanding the cost and benefit of each helps to paint the larger picture. Whether you choose to have multiple vehicles, one car and a less expensive alternate or to forego automobile ownership altogether, understanding the options available is an important first step.

Fuel

With gas prices rising, alternative fuels, hybrids and electric cars begin to look like viable options. With such a range of options out there it would be impossible for me to provide accurate calculations and suggestions on which choices to make. When considering these alternatives, look at how much money would be saved on gas and compare it to how much more the car costs. If total gas savings over the life of a car amount to $5,000 but the car costs $10,000 more than its fuel guzzling alternative, the efficient model isn't quite the deal it initially sounds like. If being green is more important than money, alternative fuels may be attractive despite the increased cost. But be aware of the total cost of ownership up front before making a decision.

I have relatives that have in the past driven across town to save 2 cents on a gallon of gas. While this may seem like a good idea initially, it helps to actually do a calculation. Assume you drive a car that gets 20 miles to the gallon and there is a gas station 5 miles away (10 miles after a round trip) that has gas for 5 cents cheaper than the one near your current location. If gas is $4 per gallon, the distance of 10 miles would effectively cost you half a gallon or $2 to venture out to. Assuming your tank holds 12 gallons, a fill up at a savings of 5 cents per gallon only equates to 60 cents. In this example it actually costs $1.40 to save $.05 per gallon. Add in the added time it takes to make the drive and it no longer sounds like a deal does it?

Efficiency

Tinted windows provide several benefits in warm climates making them well worth the cost. Not only do they make you look cool (which is of course extremely important) but they block sunlight and therefore heat. This actually has several different benefits. By reducing the amount of heat that comes into the car, this reduces the load on the air conditioning, which therefore reduces the amount of fuel used. By reducing direct sunlight on passengers, it helps to keep them cool and could be used to prevent skin damage assuming the tinting blocks harmful rays.

On a similar note, did you know that driving with your windows up actually increases fuel efficiency? At low speeds a cross breeze from an open window might counter the fuel used by an air conditioner. But at high speeds open windows create a very large amount of drag. Basically this means that wind is able to grab your car and push against it. This drag slows the car down and makes the engine work harder to maintain whatever speed you are driving.

The last automotive tip I have is to be sure to do regular maintenance on your car. By performing this maintenance, items that wear out over time can last longer, avoiding some expenses while also preventing costly repairs caused by poor maintenance. Also, by keeping everything running as efficiently as possible and keeping the tire pressure correct, significant gas savings can be realized.

With technology changes, efficiency breakthroughs and financing options changing all the time, car tips can be difficult to pin down. Hopefully the information provided in this chapter has helped to change the way you think about car ownership.

16 – Free Services

There are a surprising number of free items in the world. Many times the same goods or services are available from one company for a fee and another company for free. By spending time looking for alternatives to everything you need, you can avoid paying unnecessary fees.

Banking

Banking is a prime example of a service that benefits from shopping around. Some charge for checking, others offer it for free. Interest rates on different types of savings accounts vary greatly from one bank to another. Even the products offered are different from bank to bank with some offering money saving product bundles.

Many banks offer ATMs that can be used without a fee. However, using an out of network ATM will usually result in a fee. Some banks actually offer accounts that will refund that fee charged by out of network ATMs. Obviously the best idea would be to use the ATMs you know are already free but an offer of reimbursement can increase convenience when an in network option is far away.

Simply searching for a bank near home with the lowest costs, highest return on savings and best convenience options can make a big difference in fees paid as well as interest accrued. Try looking around and comparing your current services with options from other providers nearby.

Estimates

Many companies offer free estimates for any potential work performed. Thankfully, this trend is now more common than charging a fee for an estimate, but fees can still be found so be on the lookout. Unfortunately companies do tend to take advantage of free or reduced cost initial services in order to execute what's known as a "bait and switch". The concept is that they will offer an extremely low price for a service then find ways to up charge or add additional fees once the work has begun. While I have had many companies attempt this, the easiest example for the average American will most likely be automotive brake replacement. The allure of a low priced brake replacement brings you in, but once the car is in the air with the wheels and brakes removed, the technician points out that you will need more expensive brakes and a few new parts in order for the change to be effective.

To be fair, many times issues cannot be seen initially but become apparent once work has begun. So avoid jumping to the conclusion that the costs are unnecessary before asking a few questions. The important thing is to determine which is a bait and switch and which is a real problem in need of additional funding. Being an informed consumer can make a big difference.

Some companies actually offer free or discounted future services if products are purchased from them. A local carpet cleaning service I have used offers discounted re-cleans for a year after the initial cleaning. A local tire replacement shop offers free flat repairs and tire rotation for as long as I own the tires. A local sandwich shop offers discounted refills for buying a souvenir cup. Services like this can reduce long terms costs and should therefore always be factored in before a vendor is chosen.

A comprehensive list of the scenarios and correct decisions would be impossible to compile. But getting familiar with the concepts provided in this chapter and attempting to apply them in everyday life will be a benefit in any situation. Shopping around, receiving free quotes, asking questions and choosing services that keep on providing benefits are habits that will benefit you for a lifetime.

City Services

States, cities, counties, churches and other government or community entities provide a number of free or inexpensive services to citizens. While some are paid for by taxes, they do not necessarily require an additional fee to take advantage of.

Parks, playgrounds and lakes are just a few of the entertainment possibilities provided for free by many of these entities. Some child oriented restaurants even provide indoor playground structures that can be used any time you visit their store. While state or federal parks typically require some form of entry fee, local parks are usually free and contain things like playgrounds, soccer fields or just wide open spaces great for throwing a ball or flying a kite.

Long ago, back in the "olden days" and before the internet there was a place that housed thousands of free books. These could be borrowed for a period of time, read and returned as frequently as you desired. The name of this magical wonderland was the "Library" and yes these establishments are still around today. While the internet has definitely increased convenience, it has unfortunately caused many to forget some of the valuable local services like libraries that are still available. Not only can you get free entertainment or educational books, some libraries offer story time for kids or even the ability to check out movies on DVD.

Besides being cheap or free and convenient, reading library books expands your mind. After all, isn't that what you are doing right now? If you have kids, allow them to make decisions while having fun and learning by letting them browse library shelves to pick one or two books to check out. They will not only enjoy the stories but also get a sense of pride from making their own decisions.

Another service provided to just about everyone in America is water. Tap water is regulated, water test information is readily available and it even contains fluoride which is great for your teeth. Fluoride reduces cavities which will helps to improve the smile you will have after saving so much money from the tips in this book! Water from the tap is also dramatically cheaper than its bottled alternative, yet bottled water has become more and more common in society.

In my previous home, the tap water provided by the local water provider tasted great. By adding a filter to my refrigerator it tasted even better and was always cold and ready to drink. This led my wife and I to drink it exclusively and avoid bottled water as much as possible. Doing so provides a low cost alternative to bottled water and eliminates waste that would have resulted from using disposable bottles. By picking up a few large stainless steel water bottles from a local store, refilling them often and carrying them with us everywhere we go, we not only save money but drink more water as well.

This worked great for a while until we moved to another house in a neighboring city. The new house has very soft water with an odd taste to it right out of the tap. I made an effort to get used to the new flavor but was never able to and finally gave up. This unfortunately resulted in me reverting back to bottled water on a regular basis and spending a lot more money in the process. While I could still fill my large water bottle at the gym or at work, I was spending around $20 per month on gallons of bottled water. Knowing I was wasting money, creating plastic waste and having to haul heavy water bottles home from the store bothered me the entire time. So finally I decided to look for additional water filtration options that could make the taste of tap water pleasant again. In the end I found a filtered pitcher from Brita (www.brita.com) that successfully improved the taste with disposable filters that could be replaced about every 2 months. It still isn't as cheap as drinking straight out of a faucet, but it is less than bottled, readily available and allows me to produce less waste while drinking more water.

Software

In today's technology driven society, you probably interact with multiple pieces of software each day. Smart phones, laptops, personal computers, music players and GPS devices all use some form of software to run. Each of these pieces of software could come with additional costs that easily add up to large amounts. The trick here is to avoid paying for applications or software that could be obtained for free with a little bit of searching.

Many internet service providers (ISPs) offer free services such as email. Thankfully this has become common enough that paid email is rare outside of the corporate world. But if you do currently pay, look for alternative options. Your internet service provider is one source, but companies such as Google (www.gmail.com), Yahoo (mail.yahoo.com) and Microsoft (www.outlook.com) also offer free email services that do not disappear if you change service providers. Since moving and shopping for better deals on services could easily cause free ISP accounts to disappear, these online offerings can be very convenient over time.

Speaking of companies offering free software services, Google is currently well known for a variety of free products. The free Android operating system they created has become a widely used product on smart phones and tablets in recent years. Assuming you have internet connectivity via cellular service or Wi-Fi, Google also provides a series of applications that will guide you to almost any destination for free.

Google Maps and Google Navigation are free replacements for something many people used to pay for – GPS navigation. Not too long ago several companies offered devices that were either part of your vehicle or could be mounted on the dash or window. These devices provided voice guided directions to a destination while you drove. But, since many of these did not connect to the internet while in use, they had to be updated frequently while connected to a computer and those updates were expensive.

With Google's free navigation apps and similar offerings from Apple that update real time and offer these same services for free, car mounted, disconnected devices have almost become obsolete. Thankfully no one I know misses the old devices as these new options provide easier, up to date directions for free! Of course this assumes you have a smart phone with a data plan which does come with a substantial fee. If you already have one, this will be a great option. If not, weigh the cost of a smart phone and data plan to alternatives before making a decision.

Another product offered for free by Google is one called Google Docs (http://www.google.com/docs/about/). This is online software for word processing, spreadsheets and slide presentation. Another similar option that is also open source is Open Office (www.openoffice.org). Using either of these allows the creation of documents compatible with paid programs from Microsoft such as Word, PowerPoint and Excel without the associated fees. Considering the high cost of those products for personal use, these free options have been increasing in popularity.

For those of you interested in digital artwork or if you desire something like Adobe's Photoshop without the high cost (http://www.adobe.com/products/photoshop.html), there are a few options out there that can offer some graphic editing capabilities for free. The two I am most familiar with are Paint.net (www.getpaint.net) and GIMP (www.gimp.org). Both offer a high level of digital design capability but are open source and free.

Entertainment

Music was a hot topic a few years back when file sharing software like Napster was found to be breaching copyright laws. While that was unfortunate, the attention it received forced a change in how the music industry viewed the offerings it provided. Today we have several free software options that allow a wide variety of audio entertainment. Beyond the standard air wave radio there are also options such as Pandora (www.pandora.com) and Rdio (www.rdio.com). These allow you to select certain genres, artists or categories of music to stream for free in either a web browser or via an app on a smart phone or tablet. Typically some form of advertising is included in free services like these but they offer a great improvement over standard radio because you are allowed to tailor music to your desires. Pandora even learns what you like and plays items from artists it thinks will suit your taste. Participating in services like these not only provides free entertainment, but can also expose you to experiences you may otherwise have missed.

Not interested in music? These services also offer alternative listening options such as comedy. When stuck in traffic and unable to find something on the radio, a random laugh may be just the thing needed to pass the time.

Cable television has become very common in households across the US. But did you know local channels still broadcast programming over the air? In years past this was done with small antennas lovingly referred to as "rabbit ears". But with the right high def antenna, these over air broadcasts can even provide high definition television without a monthly fee of any kind.

For on demand programming, try out an online option such as Hulu (www.hulu.com). This company offers free current season television shows online and on demand. It does include commercials that cannot be skipped but that's a small price to pay for the convenience. Some television channel providers even offer free episodes on their website. As I'm writing this, channels such as Comedy Central (www.comedycentral.com) and NBC (www.nbc.com) are offering their shows online for free. Check out the websites of your favorite channels to see if shows of interest are available.

YouTube (www.youtube.com) is another free online video site that contains user submitted videos. Sometimes these can include older movies or television programs but a majority of the videos are home grown. This includes reviews, opinions, how to and informational videos, as well as a wide variety of random entertainment. I personally have found the wide array of how to videos to be extremely useful. Just recently I had a window that had come off of its track. Rather than hire a window professional to come out and provide a repair estimate, I was able to hop onto YouTube, find an instructional video and make the repairs myself. So beyond just providing free entertainment, this site can reduce costs for a do it yourselfer as well!

17 – Kids

Kids are a never ending source of love and joy that everyone should have at some point in life. With this joy comes a very large financial responsibility that needs to be taken seriously. Not just with the amount of money that raising children requires but also the responsibility of teaching the next generation how to save and spend wisely. By reading this book you have taken the first step, so let me continue with additional tips related directly to kids.

Cost Savings

It is important to note that without proper planning, kids have the potential to be bottomless money pits. The good news is that the expense of raising children does not have to be nearly as high as many families make it. From birth through the toddler years, all children have certain similar needs that require mild use of products with a long lifespan. By attempting to find these products either used or as hand me downs from friends or family, huge amounts of money can be saved. To get an idea of what I am referring to, examine the following list.

- High chair
- Booster seat
- Pack and play
- Walker
- Clothing
- Baby, toddler or transition beds
- Bedding
- Toys
- Books
- Strollers
- Room decor

These products can be purchased at large discounts from a variety of places such as resale shops, garage sales or websites like eBay (www.ebay.com) or Craigslist (www.craigslist.org). Local discount stores typically store the most common items while garage sales and Craigslist can have hidden gems for amazing prices. Websites like eBay can be a mixed bag. While they are almost guaranteed to have anything you could possibly be interested in, prices vary greatly. Years ago auction sites were used as public garage sales where people interested in selling unused items were brought together with a large base of interested buyers. These days small business owners have joined in, which has increased the available selection, but also driven up prices.

Hand me downs are possibly the most difficult but least expensive items to find. If family members, close friends or even coworkers have children that are a year or two older than yours, they may have plenty of items to hand down to your kids. By passing on the favor to someone else when your kids are done with those items, as well as adding a few you may have bought, another family will reap the benefits too. By passing down items to them, they will be encouraged to pass items on to the next family therefore creating a chain of savings. In an age where community unity seems to be decreasing, helping your neighbor is a refreshing change.

Whether you manage to find a source of hand me downs, free gifts or just find great deals on used or discounted items be sure to think long term. If an item of clothing is too large for your child, hold on to it as kids grow fast. If a toy is meant for a different age group, put it in a closet until your child reaches that age. If your child simply has too many toys because of all the wonderful deals you have found, put a few aside to be used as Christmas or birthday presents. By thinking long term you can take advantage of deals throughout the year even if there is not an immediate need for them.

One of the most interesting things I noticed in raising my two children was how each of them showed interest in different types of toys. Toys my daughter had never touched became my son's favorite. Toys by daughter loved were of no interest to my son. Some of the toys they had were never played with at all as neither child showed an interest. Had I bought all of their toys new, imagine the amount of money that would have been wasted and how it would have felt on those neither child showed interest in. With that in mind, I would suggest selecting toys carefully and not overextending too soon. Try out a few items to see what your child plays with more and then target additional purchases towards those categories. This is really just a matter of spending wisely, but savings can really add up when doing so while also buying used.

Another area where my wife and I focused with our kids during the pre-teeth years was food. Prepared baby food from the store is surprisingly expensive and creates lots of waste. By using a food processor to puree fresh fruits and vegetables, our children ate very cheaply and more naturally than they would have by eating store bought baby food. I have even heard store bought baby food compared to dog food in the past. I cannot attest to the true health facts or ingredient content of these items but when meals are prepared from scratch I know for sure what they contain. Combining that with the large cost savings achieved from this method made me a very happy father.

Teaching

Once you have mastered the tips provided for decreasing expenses, it is time to move on to teaching your kids what you have learned. At some point in life, everyone must learn the basics of economics. Producing goods, providing services, bartering, saving, spending and other concepts are very important but do not necessarily come naturally. If your kids are taught these ideas early on in life, they will be better prepared when eventually moving out and making ends meet on their own.

The area my parents live in has become highly sought after by affluent families with very high incomes. According to my parents, far too many of those wealthy parents provide everything for their kids and do not place much emphasis on finances or saving and spending habits. When a 16 year old needs their first car, they are not provided with a safe, used option. Instead they are given brand new luxury SUVs. Instead of shopping sales and discount racks, the kids are allowed to purchase all new, brand name clothing. Concepts of reusing, repurposing and recycling are foreign to these kids. The end result has been high school graduates with an unrealistic expectation about the quality of life they can expect for a hard day's work. They look at the Joneses as a typical American family and assume their lifestyle should match.

After attending college, moving out and seeing the real world, many of these young adults become what are known as "Boomerang Kids". Basically that just means they were not equipped to make it on their own and therefore ended up moving back in with Mom and Dad to re-enable the lifestyle they were accustomed to. While this could be a joy for empty nesters, the job of parents is to teach kids everything they need to know in order to make it in life. If these kids come back home, parents did not do their jobs effectively.

Teaching financial responsibility does not have to be a large, boring and time consuming process for parents. Instead, it can be a fun and exciting way to use your imagination. I have very fond memories growing up of playing grocery store with my siblings. Some of us would be the tellers with a stash of toys creating our imaginary inventory. The others would carry toy coins, marbles, rocks or other imaginary forms of currency. We would browse the wares, selecting what we wanted, then have fun calculating which form of imaginary currency was worth more and how much change should be given. As in real life, whichever was most rare became the most valuable.

This may just sound like kids playing and to be honest, it was. But during these games we were learning valuable concepts without even knowing it. Determining that the small quantity of red marbles were worth more than the large quantity of white ones was a hidden lesson in supply and demand. Calculating change was a hidden math lesson as well as an experience in spending choices. Choosing several items that required very few marbles resulted in a large remainder of our currency as well as the ability to acquire more for less. The alternative could have been to spend all of our marbles, rocks, toy coins and other currency on a single, really cool toy. But that decision meant we would only have the one toy to play with. Making lessons into games like this is great for children of all ages and kids will usually expand the game ideas on their own.

While at a garage sale a few years ago, I came across a toy cash register. It contained a calculator, receipt area and a drawer to hold money. At a different garage sale as well as a local store, I found sets of play money including dollars, coins and a cash tray. While the trays do not fit in the drawer of the cash register, the combination of these two toys provides me with a great series of lessons for my kids. With actual bills and coins that mimic real currency and a working, calculating cash register, we practice buying items, calculating change and understanding how spending affects savings or residual cash.

I even managed to find toy checks on a dollar rack at one local store. With credit cards so prominent, checks are not nearly as common as they used to be, but these have already provided wonderful entertainment for my daughter. I cannot begin to describe the joy of having a 4 year old write a check for hugs and kisses. In later years these can be used to teach real lessons about checking accounts and deferred methods of payment. But for now I plan on enjoying the free affection.

The first lesson we taught my daughter was about earning money for providing a service. She was offered the opportunity to earn a quarter each time her play room was picked up. Initially this was a hard sell. After all, what good was money to a child? But one day we went to the store where she saw a singing and talking toy dog that she absolutely had to have. In this case it was a stuffed dog named Violet made by Leap Frog (www.leapfrog.com). At the time this toy cost around $20 and we were not willing to fork over that kind of money for something that would most likely end up unused on a shelf. Thus began our opportunity to teach a life lesson about money.

My wife and I reminded our daughter about how she could earn money by cleaning her playroom each day and that in time, that money would add up to enough to buy Violet herself. That was the trigger she needed. For months my daughter would diligently clean up her toys and excitedly add quarters to her a plastic bag we had hung on the refrigerator. This location was important because having a transparent container in a highly visible location created a constant reminder of the growing funds. Occasionally we would sit her down to count the quarters and offer to exchange them for dollars. Each time this was done we asked how many quarters made a dollar, to which she would excitedly answer "four!" Once the conversion was complete, she would help us count out the dollars and then determine how much more was needed before Violet could be purchased. Now keep in mind, we are loving parents so extra money would mysteriously sneak its way into that bag every so often. But that did not take away from the underlying lesson. After a few months of this I noticed something very interesting. My daughter's enthusiasm for this toy had not diminished. By having a goal that she was saving up for, her interest in the toy was increasing as the anticipation built.

Eventually she had enough saved, so we made a big deal out of a trip to the store to buy the toy she had put so much effort into saving up for. We let her pick the one she wanted off of the shelf, sit with it in the cart and even pay for it at the register. Seeing a child hand over her own money to a cashier to purchase her very own toy is a moment you will never forget. Not only was this rewarding for everyone involved, but my daughter learned several valuable lessons. Working to earn money, saving up over time, anticipation of an exciting new toy and patience were just a few of the concepts she was introduced to. Also, the toy I had expected to end up on a shelf became her favorite possession that she never left home without.

A valuable lesson found in this exercise is to avoid buying on impulse. You might remember this from a previous chapter but seeing it in practice is helpful. In the beginning of the story I mentioned the fear of buying an item that would sit on a shelf. All too often in my house if an item is bought on impulse it does end up just sitting on a shelf and forgotten about. Yet by waiting, ensuring the item is necessary and building anticipation, the item ended up as a valuable and useful purchase. While this lesson is very important for adults to learn, it is even more important for children. Marketing teams across the world are tasked with encouraging consumers to buy their products and a very easy target for them is children.

Spend an afternoon watching your child's favorite television channel. Pay special attention to the commercials that come on and see if you notice a pattern. Commercials targeted towards children are energetic, very colorful and always display other kids having a great time playing with whatever is being sold. It is now an ongoing joke in my house when a commercial comes on that my daughter will, without exception say "I want that!" Then in the same breath as one commercial ends and another begins will say "I want that too!" She has now been conditioned to expect a response of "You just want everything!" with a chuckle as we have never bought anything for her from a commercial. But the point is that the marketing works. Kids are attracted to those commercials and immediately want whatever is being sold. In my house it doesn't even appear to matter what the item is my kids want, it is simply because the commercial convinced them of that fact.

The reason this lesson is important to learn early in life is because of how great a job marketing teams do in selling to adults as well. Taking those same commercials as an example, did you see these other common themes?

"If you buy now, we'll also throw in X, Y AND Z!"

"But wait, there's more!"

"And that's not all! We're going to double your order!"

"And for a limited time you also get the free supermathingy!"

"All for just 3 easy payments of $19.99!"

So here's what is happening. The goal of all of the statements above is to trigger a feeling that the item in question is suddenly a great deal while emphasizing the importance of an immediate impulse purchase. From a child's perspective, a colorful and exciting display is all that's needed to be convinced the item is worth buying. But adults typically have been conditioned to expect and ignore some of that excitement. So the next step is to target a different emotion by using several strategies to make the item sound like a great deal. This can be very effective if not expected. By teaching both lessons to your children as early as possible, they will be conditioned to ignore both marketing patterns and will therefore be able to make logical financial decisions in any situation.

Do you remember bell bottom or flare leg pants? How about Furbies (www.furby.com), Beanie Babies (www.ty.com) or Tickle Me Elmo (www.hasbro.com)? All of these items were either brand name sensations or fad items with a huge amount of interest over a short period of time followed by quickly diminishing interest. Had you been one of the unfortunate parents paying well over sticker price for Christmas presents or buying current, stylish clothing that would embarrass your child the next year you would have wasted plenty of money. Recognizing items that are simply overpriced current fads that will soon fade and explaining how trends like this work, is very important to the development of your child. There will always be a new, hot item that will make your child the coolest kid in school. There will always be an item that was "so last year". Explaining these concepts while displaying alternatives is a great way for your child to learn the value of money.

This can be difficult when schools have children from other families like the Joneses. Many other children will be wearing the latest fashion trends or own the new and improved Widget 3000. Peer pressure will then encourage your child to follow the rest and Mr. Rich's strategies will begin to look boring by comparison. In these cases having a few tricks up your sleeve will come in handy.

When your child really wants the latest, expensive fashion item, start by showing an assortment of other, less expensive items in order to quantify all they could have for the same price. Try using the example of Mr. Rich versus The Joneses in the Coupons, Sales and Discounts chapter about purchasing clothing to explain the concept. Sometimes allowing a single splurge item with other discount purchases can teach the same lesson. When your child begins to find that one item falling out of style, they will begin to see the value of everything else that was bought at the same time. This could apply to clothing, toys or any other category. It will also provide a lesson in moderation which is the most important concept for children to learn but also the best strategy you will have for teaching.

Moderation is a very powerful tool in your arsenal of educational tactics. It effectively allows your children to have some of what they want, limits overall consumption and provides a lesson in alternatives with minimal pushback. Typically in my household this is used when my kids decide that treats provide all the sustenance needed to survive. By enforcing the idea that treats are a sometimes food that can only be enjoyed if the rest of their food is eaten, they start to learn good habits. Carrying this same logic into purchases, allowing a treat can be an equally effective educational tool. If your child finds several items on the discount rack, allow them a single, expensive splurge. Agreements like this save you money, prevent arguments and teach valuable lessons for the future.

There are a few more very important topics to teach kids that are much more difficult than those presented so far. These involve long term and conceptual topics that of course are difficult for young minds to comprehend. These are learning to save and the value of interest.

I remember a time in elementary school when my siblings and I received a small allowance. I would typically save it until I found some candy then spend everything while proceeding into a cavity inducing evening of consumption. My sister on the other hand, would save everything in her piggy bank and was very good about not touching it. One sunny afternoon, we heard the familiar song of the ice cream truck echoing through our neighborhood. Excited as we always were to hear that sound, we grabbed our savings and ran to the curb. Unfortunately, I had very little saved and was not able to buy anything. My sister on the other hand was sitting on a small fortune and was able to buy the best thing on the menu. I remember a feeling of jealousy as well as a sense of injustice. I did not understand why she was able to get something that I was not.

This is truly a problem for kids. Cause and effect over a period of time is a difficult concept to understand when you are young. While your kids might not get it at first, this is something that is extremely important to teach. By giving the same lesson repeatedly and enforcing the concept over time, it will slowly begin to sink in. With my daughter, the first lesson was simply to save for a specific toy. It was a targeted lesson that did not involve generic saving but rather saving for something specific. I highly suggest using targeted lessons in the beginning. Once those seem to be understood, then move on to general savings.

General savings is going to involve two primary concepts. The first is to put a portion of what is made into savings without having a plan to spend those funds on anything. The next will be to put those funds into a savings account and explain how they can accrue interest over time.

A good rule of thumb is to have your child put 10% of everything made aside. This could be money received as gifts for Christmas or birthdays, allowance or cash earned for some specific task such as babysitting. Regardless of the source, setting up a pattern of always saving that 10% is the important part, as it will create a routine that will carry into adulthood.

This is easier said than done of course. Imagine this from the perspective of a young mind. When a child receives $10 and is told that $1 must be put away and not used the following questions may come up.

"You want me to do what?"

"But it's my money I want to buy some candy!"

"When do I get to spend the savings?"

"But I promise I won't ask for another toy if you just let me spend all of my money now."

"But I need it now!"

Responses to those questions and statements will vary greatly depending on the personality of the child. My strong willed daughter requires a full explanation of everything, several rounds of the question "Why?" with an eventual "just because I said so!" to complete the discussion. While you could attempt to use interest, or rather the idea that by putting money away it will grow, as a motivator. But since that will also be difficult for them to understand, your results will vary. Even so, it is important to begin a habit of saving as early as possible. While it will be a battle, it will begin to make sense whenever the accrued savings are actually used to buy something expensive. That will be the "Ah ha!" moment for your child where they see the fruits of their labor result in an amazing reward. Watching that realization materialize will feel amazing as a parent.

Allowance

Allowance is a hotly debated topic in many families as it can be a powerful teaching tool but also a hindrance if used incorrectly. The two areas of contention are usually how much money to give each allowance cycle and what must be done during that cycle to earn it. Must all chores be done in order to receive it? Would that teach kids to only do chores if they get paid? If your child is given too much money will it limit their ability to understand the value of a dollar? All of these and more could come up when discussing this topic with your significant other.

Once again moderation will be the answer on how to tie chores to an allowance. If all chores translate to money, children could very well end up only helping out when they are paid for time. If allowance is just a free gift, children will never understand the value of that money. If allowance and work are completely separate, it will be very difficult to motivate a child to do anything. To that end I suggest creating 2 categories of chores. One category will simply be ongoing chores that must be done as a member of the family without any kind of reward. The other category will be those that must be done in order to receive an allowance.

The chores that must be complete without reward will eventually translate to ongoing tasks that must be completed by adults. Those would include cleaning house, taking out the trash, paying bills, car maintenance, etc. These are all tasks that adults must participate in but do not provide any kind of monetary reward. The chores that are tied to an allowance will translate to a primary job, side job or even contracting work that adults may find. By simply creating these two categories at a young age, children will understand that separation later in life. While children of the Joneses will grow up expecting to receive something for nothing, yours will grow up understanding the value of a hard day's work. This will create the internal drive necessary to become Mr. Rich later in life if they so choose.

Quantity of an allowance depends on what you provide for free and the cost of living in your area. In my area, starting out at ¼ a child's pre teen age per week and moving up to ½ or a full teen's age per week is a good plan. At an age of 6, this would mean $1.50 per week. That could buy candy or a cheap toy each week or could be saved for a month to buy something larger. At an age of 14, that would provide $7 to $14 per week. Obviously if you provide all meals, snacks and entertainment and live in an area with a very low cost of living $7 per week would be plenty. If your child must pay for any treats or entertainment or you live in an area where things are more expensive the larger amount will make more sense.

In either case the important thing is to start low and stick to a calculation. If you accidentally provide an allowance early on that is too much, it will be very difficult to decrease the amount without receiving a large amount of pushback. Imagine suddenly getting a pay cut at work because your boss feels you are paid too much! On the flip side of that is starting out with a low expectation then getting a surprise raise. By starting low you will always have the ability to raise the allowance at any time and your child will love it.

The beauty of using age in your calculation is that it sets a future expectation that kids can look forward to. Rather than constantly asking for a raise, they know when the next one is due to arrive. Hopefully this will work as a lesson in patience and anticipation but regardless, a birthday raise is a great gift your kids will look forward to year after year.

An allowance can also be a great way to teach kids about savings without having to wait for cash to arrive as gifts for

Christmas or birthdays. Those events happen only twice a year while an allowance is usually a weekly event. By applying the 10% rule to an allowance, money will be saved each week and the lesson will be taught consistently over a period of time.

The last thing I find important about an allowance is that it teaches responsibility and allows kids to learn that concept at their own pace. Kids are responsible for doing the chores necessary to earn the allowance. They are also responsible for the money set aside in savings from the allowance each week. They determine what the spendable cash is used for and they get to put the savings into the container or account each week. This is very empowering and can be a wonderful educational experience.

18 – Value vs. Cost

Everyone loves a good deal, but what exactly makes something a deal or makes it a good value for the cost? Is it simply a low price? How about something that lasts a long time? Maybe something with a very long warranty that includes free replacement? Are cheap items always a good value? Does more expensive always mean better? Have you ever really sat down and thought this through? The following exercise will be very revealing.

Using the form on the next page, come up with a list of scenarios you have encountered in which you felt a purchase made ended up being a great value for the price. Add a short explanation for each of the items. Once those are complete, think about situations you encountered where you felt a purchase ended up not being a great value for the price. Add in a short explanation there as well. Once complete, continue on for a detailed look at how value and cost relate.

Great Value	Not A Value

Did any interesting patterns become apparent in this exercise? If not, allow me to elaborate a bit on what might have been found. Typically a low price instantly attracts potential buyers to an item simply because it costs less regardless of the quality. In years past a higher price usually meant something was of a better quality. Unfortunately as time goes by, I find that price seems to be less and less related to the actual quality of an item. I have frequently found inexpensive items that did not even perform the task they were built to perform. In those cases, the cost of the item was irrelevant. Any price paid for an item that does not do what it should is too much. On the other hand, I have also paid for more expensive items under the assumption that they would provide years of quality use only to have them break down in the first few weeks. Similarly I have eaten at gourmet restaurants at great expense only to leave unsatisfied and craving inexpensive fast food. These experiences have brought the realization that these days cheap sometimes just means low quality junk and expensive sometimes just means overpriced.

This is where the concept of value comes in. I view value as the return on investment received whenever an item is purchased. By paying $5 for a tool, will I receive $5 worth of use out of that too? By paying $10 for the same tool made by a different manufacturer, will I receive double the value versus buying the $5 version? This value can take many forms. It could be usability of a product, lifespan of a product, taste of a consumable, or even whether an emergency item actually works when you have a need for it in an emergency situation.

With the experiences you listed in the previous exercise, how many items were listed as not being a value when the price was very low? These would be examples of those that either broke on the first use, tasted horrible, did not perform their intended purpose or simply did not live up to expectations. How many of those items listed as not a value were actually expensive? These would include anything that cost more than an available alternative but did not perform better or taste better or provide an overall better experience than the cheaper alternative would have.

The important takeaway here is that the value of an item is not necessarily tied to the cost and that buyers must take care to avoid wasting money on items that will not provide the value necessary to justify their cost. Thankfully there is a now a widespread utility at your fingertips to assist with this process. This tool is called an online review and has become prevalent in retailers everywhere.

Reviews

Whether shopping in a brick and mortar store or online, reviews are a handy item to rely on. When in a store, a quick search on a smart phone can provide hundreds of reviews containing details on the quality of whatever you are interested in purchasing. When shopping online, a second browser window can provide an even more convenient method of finding this information. Not only that, many times users writing reviews also include alternative items they have tried. This could either lead you to make the purchase knowing it comes highly recommended or to have a change of heart and instead research alternatives that were suggested.

Since many different companies sell the same products, reviews can often be found for a product you're interested in at the website of a retailer different from the one you intend to make a purchase. By using a search engine and exploring reviews across a variety of retailers, plenty of information can be found. Do not be discouraged if one website is lacking in reviews. Instead, keep searching as someone is bound to have purchased and reviewed that item before you.

This method works great for larger or more expensive items where the purchase has a larger potential for regret. Televisions, electronics, cars, tools and appliances all have great potential to be big regrets if money is wasted on the wrong one. But small items can benefit just as much. I can't even count the number of times I have considered buying something from Amazon (www.amazon.com) only to find a review that says "It's much smaller than I expected" or "It broke the first time I used it". Reviews like those have encouraged me to look for alternatives many times, which in turn made the shopping experience that much more enjoyable. When the final order was placed, I was always confident in what was bought.

Another popular tool commonly advertised is Angie's List (www.angieslist.com). This website provides reviews on companies that provide services rather than products. When looking for a company to provide a service, an incorrect choice could not only result in regret, but also additional expenses. Time after time I have had friends complain of a contractor hired to do some work that was left unfinished. Fixing the mistakes that contractor made and finishing the work ended up costing more than a reputable company would have charged in the first place. Had they put forth some additional effort up front to hire someone with positive reviews rather than jump on the lowest price, money could have been saved and stress avoided. Just like with products, the lowest price does not always mean the best deal.

Sometimes the ability to look for reviews is not available. This could be for items that simply do not have reviews, an impulse buy from a clearance rack, lack of internet connectivity, lack of time or the lack of an alternative product. A great example of these items could be those advertised as deals for Black Friday (the Friday after Thanksgiving). Companies notoriously promote deals that appear too good to be true on items that do not have reviews. For those, you must just use judgment based on experience to determine whether the purchase will live up to expectations.

Scams

It would be wise to remember that anything appearing to be "too good to be true" usually is. In the case of Black Friday deals, retailers pull several tricks to sway unsuspecting customers. The easiest of these is the fine print that states "limited quantities". I have personally been to a store with an advertised Black Friday special where the store did not even have the item advertised in stock when the doors opened. In that case "limited quantities" meant it was limited across the company, not per store. The other trick I see most often is that of a special, limited production electronic item such as televisions. The Black Friday special will look just like another higher priced item in the store just with a lower price. But upon closer inspection, the lower priced item will actually contain fewer features and therefore have less value.

For me, the end result here is that I avoid the hype of Black Friday and just stay home. My purchases are all well thought out, planned in advance and thoroughly reviewed beforehand. While this means I never experience the Black Friday "deals", the questionable nature of those deals make it something I do not miss.

A questionable practice found in a few local retailers near me recently was that of large percentage off sales. While the specifics vary, it was usually a variety of the same idea that the entire store was 40%, 50%, 60%, etc off. The truth in a recent and revealing news article was that the stores would actually mark up their items the night before a sale then mark them down 40%, 50% or 60% off of the marked up price. One product I remember hearing about ended up with a sale price higher than the original unmodified price was. Thankfully by shopping around, being prepared and understanding the true value of an item, scams like this can be easily avoided.

Insurance

Insurance is another foggy option to be negotiated. Reading and understanding the fine print will be your best tool when comparing insurance providers and policies. Insurance policies are complicated, so I will break down the most important items I look at when shopping around, from most important to least important.

1. Does the provider have good reviews?
2. Does the provider pay out easily when a claim is made?
3. Does the policy cover everything you think it will cover?
4. What is the sweet spot of deductible to policy premium? Usually a balance can be found that provides the best bang for your buck.

As usual my top suggestion is to look for reviews. Right after that is whether the provider pays out when a claim is made. This can easily be compared to the question about products when wondering if they will actually fulfill their intended purpose. Just like with products, if the intended purpose cannot be filled, any amount of money is too much. But in this, case needing to file a claim and being denied or even just postponed endlessly can be worse than paying a higher premium at a more reputable company.

The third item in the list is tricky. Each policy covers something different and sometimes a minor detail in the fine print can result in a denied claim. This could be something like flood damage, hail damage, earthquake damage or in the case of health insurance, it could be a medication you need that is not covered. Recently there was an incident at a home on a nearby lake where the ground fell out from under part of the home. The insurance provider did not cover "ground movement" and therefore denied the family's claim. Imagine losing your house over something like that.

A less severe consequence I dealt with a few years back was with a medication prescribed by my doctor. The doctor had prescribed a certain quantity for treatment, but the insurance company limited the quantity to half of the prescription. The end result was that I would have to pay two separate co-pays in order to receive the full dose. This was more of an annoyance rather than a detriment, but it does display how something minor could quickly escalate into a major expense purely based on some unexpected fine print.

The last item in the list is simply a matter of cost comparison. Usually each policy comes with a premium or monthly payment, as well as a deductible. Deductibles are the amount you must pay out of pocket before insurance will kick in. While paying a deductible is never fun, it can be beneficial. I once had a situation with my car insurance where reducing my deductible from $500 to $100 would increase my 6 month premium by $400. It was cheaper to leave the $500 deductible, as the lower option would have forced me to pay the difference every 6 months. Since I do not make claims twice a year, the choice was easy. It will not always be so obvious, but realizing a sweet spot exists will be beneficial in your search for a happy medium.

Name Brand

Name brand versus generic is a common argument that can fall into the cost versus value category. As with all things, the answer is somewhere in the middle. Some brands are more expensive because they have a history of creating reliable, consistent and quality items. Choosing a cheaper alternative will most likely result in a lower quality. Others are simply overpriced because they are associated with a celebrity or are well known. Basically the name itself increases the price. Knowing the difference can help you make better decisions and possibly save money.

I have even run into situations where buying a high quality brand that will last does not make sense. Craftsman (www.craftsman.com) is a well known brand of tools that has for years offered lifetime replacement on things like screwdrivers. While that is great for some people, if you're like me and accidentally misplace screwdrivers all the time, buying a discount brand might very well make more sense.

At this point we begin to enter the realm of situational decisions. The value of an item can vary depending on the circumstance, situation or personal preference. Water in the desert will be a whole lot more valuable at any price than it would in a flood. By pointing out the differences, I hope to equip you to think things through before taking action. The process of stopping, thinking, comparing and then making a decision will usually result in a better choice than impulse alone would have.

19 – Cut costs

So far we have covered a variety of conceptual topics with an array of examples to increase understanding. With the core concepts of financial stability well in hand, we can discuss some additional cost saving tips to help refine a plan for future spending. To that end, I have gathered up a wide range of cost saving suggestions that can be used in day to day life, which will aid in the quest to living within your means.

Buying Used

It is always fun to bring home something shiny and new from a store. But often times these products end up being used for only a portion of their lifespan. By looking for these items used, you can reduce the cost of each by effectively sharing the lifespan with someone else.

Video games are products I love to buy used. These can be found at stores like GameStop (www.gamestop.com), on websites like Craigslist or eBay as well as locally from a friend or family member. The games and consoles last a very long time but the entertainment value of some games lasts for only a single run through. By purchasing a game used and reselling it when you are done you effectively share the lifespan and cost of the game with others. The end result feels like a very inexpensive rental without a time constraint.

As discussed in the Kids chapter, toys are wonderful items to purchase used. Most quality toys are very durable and can last for years while the age group those toys are meant for may span only a matter months. This results in what marketing teams love to call "gently used merchandise". The reality is that the items were only used a little bit, are still in great shape and still have plenty of life left in them. Even those items meant for large age ranges can be great deals used. Bicycles, scooters, board games, puzzles and Legos (www.lego.com) last so long they can actually be passed from generation to generation. I still have Legos from my childhood to which I have added many more sets. As my kids grow, they will continue to build amazing creations with them.

The same can be said for various types of gas powered vehicles. With a little care and ongoing maintenance, things like cars, boats, motorcycles, scooters, go karts, motor homes or ATVs can last for 20 years or more! Since most items begin losing value immediately after being purchased new, buying one a few years old can save quite a bit of money while still allowing many years of enjoyment.

Some might question the ability of items to last 20 or more years. Yet I do not suggest this time frame due to wishful thinking or theory. This timeframe was actually determined based on my own personal experiences. For my 5th birthday I received a small, gas powered, 3-wheeler from my grandfather. Surprisingly enough, my wife received a 4-wheeler of the same brand and size when she was a child as well. Now over 30 years later, our family is still using both the 3-wheeler and 4-wheeler! By simply keeping them garaged and doing some minor maintenance we hope to continue getting years of enjoyment out of them. The best part is these cost us very little to continue enjoying.

Of course the longevity of these items truly depends on how well they are taken care of over the years. A used vehicle could easily end up as a money pit if the previous owner let important parts deteriorate. Understanding what you are buying and how to know whether that item is in good condition is important here.

Thankfully the amount of depreciation these items accrue in a short period of time can typically offset a few unexpected repairs. As a matter of fact, I have a friend that had always dreamed of owning a custom motorcycle. Because of that he completely ignored the used market in order to custom select everything that went into his new bike. It was fun for the first year or so but the thrill of owning the bike ended shortly thereafter. He ended up selling it for just 60% of the original purchase price when it was 2.5 years old. That was a horrible investment for him, but a great one for the buyer.

Shop Online

Shopping online can be a fast way to impulsively order things you do not need. But when used properly, it can also be a great resource for finding deals and comparing costs. Back in what my family likes to call "The Olden Days", we used to have to drive from store to store looking for places that had a particular item in stock while also hoping to find the best deal possible. This was time consuming, frustrating and used up quite a bit of gas. These days a quick search on any search engine provides instant cost comparisons and availability information at a wide variety of online retailers. Rather than driving around town looking for the best deal, that time can be spent doing something more productive.

Having these items shipped directly to your doorstep without having to leave home is a convenience I have come to love. Even if I find that a store down the street has an item in stock, by ordering online I don't have to get out of my chair! The most common downside to this is the cost of shipping. However, many times retailers offer free shipping if the total order reaches a certain amount. If not, try searching your favorite coupon code website to see if they offer a free shipping code. You may even find something better, like a code for a percentage off of the entire order. The end result could be getting the items you need shipped directly to your doorstep for the same or less than you would have paid at a retail store.

Hard to find items can actually be easier to buy online than in retail stores. During my last move, I ended up with a non-working jetted bath tub. After having a plumber come take a look and telling me he didn't know how to find a replacement part, I hopped online. After about 10 minutes of searching I found the exact part needed at a very reasonable price. Without that ability, I would have ended up searching every hardware and pool store in the area, while trying to describe the part needed.

Products in certain categories are almost always cheaper when bought online. While the categories this applies to are definitely a small portion of the overall market, understanding which items fit here can save a lot. Electronic cabling is a perfect example that always seems to be more expensive in local retail stores. This includes items such as USB, audio and video cables including VGA, DVI or HDMI. A bit of time spent searching for products of interest online will reveal which items fit into this category and which do not.

One large drawback to online ordering is when an item ordered needs to be returned. Whether it is defective, doesn't suit your needs or was even damaged in shipping, a return will be needed. Depending on the retailer this may mean lost return shipping costs and time spent repackaging and heading to a local shipping store. Thankfully many local retailers offer online shipping with free returns to their retail stores. By taking advantage of these offers, you can buy online confident in your ability to easily return the item if the need arises.

Fees

Since the Great Recession, fees have been creeping into areas where they were previously unheard of. But even before that fees were common place in many areas. From late fees to ATM fees, to those buried deep within long term service contracts, extra charges were bound to be experienced by everyone at some point. While being confronted with a fee of some sort is frustrating and often unexpected, there are ways to avoid the most common culprits.

Before the great recession the most common fee I came across was a late fee. Whether returning a movie late, paying a bill late or being late to pick up my wife and therefore paying a nag fee, being late would always result in some kind of undesired penalty. Thankfully those are easy to avoid with a little preplanning so I am usually able to succeed. There was however one unavoidable example in particular that stands out. My wife had shopped at a popular retailer one weekend that offered a discount on the entire order if she opened a store credit card. Always anxious to receive something for less, my wife accepted and the balance of the transaction was placed on the new credit account. Unbeknownst to her, the store associate had mistyped her address which resulted in my wife never receiving a bill. Since this was the first transaction, it was not clear when the bill would arrive or who to contact about it. In the end she was faced with a $25 late fee on a bill that was never received. While this fee would have been difficult to avoid, we found ourselves discussing ways to handle situations like this differently in the future. We also closed the account since we felt this retailer could no longer be trusted.

The important message here is that fees can creep up on the most honest and diligent person. So for fees that can be avoided an effort should definitely be made to do so. For ATM fees this will mean only using your bank's ATM where fees are waved. For checking accounts this could mean maintaining a minimum balance. For late fees, this will mean paying bills and returning rentals on time. For fees like tolls, this may mean planning an alternate driving route that avoids the toll. In each case the plan of execution is the same. Understand what will cause a fee then make a concerted effort to avoid it.

Unfortunately there are plenty of other more complicated fees that have appeared since the Great Recession. The most prominent in the news recently have been those imposed by airlines. On a recent flight I was charged a fee for luggage, then offered options to pay additional amounts for priority boarding and airline miles. Other airlines have even begun charging fees for water and soft drinks in flight. The best plan is to avoid these completely but that isn't always possible. In those cases simply understanding what fees may appear and finding ways around them will be your best course of action. For in flight beverages, take an empty water bottle through the security checkpoint then fill it up at a water fountain near your gate. For luggage, pack as much as possible in a carry-on and even share a suitcase if flying with someone else.

Another common fee found outside of the airline industry has been masked under the name "convenience fee". Basically this translates to a surcharge for making something available to you that otherwise would not have been. This could include an additional charge by an online payment processor, a charge for use of an in room snack bar at a hotel or even priority processing that reduces wait time. Thankfully these are very easily avoided by planning ahead. If you do not need the convenience due to appropriate planning, there will be no need to pay for the additional convenience.

The most frustrating category as well as the most difficult to avoid is the hidden fee. This could include a breach of contract fee, an additional fee a hotel charges after being booked through a travel site, or even something as ridiculous as a fuel surcharge. The latter in particular has appeared more frequently as gas prices have risen. Rather than raise the price of a service, companies have kept advertised prices the same and just appended a fuel surcharge to anything requiring gas. This keeps their prices artificially low and surprises the buyer after the initial purchase. The best defense against this is to always read the fine print. Each of these services comes with some sort of agreement that must be signed and the potential charges will be listed somewhere in that document. While these cannot always be avoided, alternate providers can be found and if everyone were to use a vendor that did not charge those fees in lieu of one that does, the message would come across loud and clear to the industry as a whole.

The most fee ridden thing my wife and I have ever encountered was a cruise. The initial price of the vacation package seemed very reasonable at first glance. It was marketed as an all inclusive vacation with food, a comfortable room and entertainment all for one low price. The reality of the trip was a different story from before we even boarded the ship. There was a fuel surcharge right up front since gas prices had recently increased. Then we were not allowed to carry our own bags to the room but instead were prompted to tip an attendant that would do it instead. From there we found that any drinks other than tea, coffee and water would require yet another fee. Being a soda addict I opted to pay for the soft drink package but the unexpected charge did not sit well.

Once the trip was underway we were confronted with a casino, overpriced alcohol and restaurants beyond the all inclusive options that required yet another fee. When arriving in a port there were plenty of excursion options at various prices as well as staff handing out bottled water if we just agreed to one more fee. Then to wrap up the trip we were informed that it was customary to spend over $100 per stateroom as tips for various staff members that provided services during our trip.

Now I must admit the trip itself was wonderful and full of memorable experiences. But to be confronted with so many unexpected fees on what was supposed to be an all inclusive vacation was a shock. We avoided most of the additional expenses by simply eating at the included restaurants, filling empty water bottles rather than buying new, foregoing alcohol and tipping only the staff that actually assisted us. Can you come up with a similar experience that was almost ruined due to a slew of unexpected fees? Once again, understanding what to expect and avoiding fees where possible is the key to enjoying these experiences while still saving money. If the total cost with fees added is higher than you're willing to pay, avoid the purchase and put the money into savings instead.

Discounts

There are plenty of discounts in the market if you know where to look. In a previous chapter I went over coupons, sales, discount cards and loyalty programs. While those are going to be the most obvious methods, there are plenty of others worth mentioning.

Most name brand products have a competitor that makes a less expensive, generic alternative. This could mean buying a store brand generic acetaminophen tablet instead of Tylenol or a generic soda instead of Coca Cola. Many stores actually have a common brand they label these less expensive items under. A few off the top of my head are Equate, Safeway Select and Great Value. These brands tend to make a less expensive version of just about everything including medicine, food and toiletries. Not all of these are equal to the name brand alternative, but by trying them out and finding those that would work as a suitable replacement, long term spending can be reduced.

Not all alternatives are what you would consider "generic". Sometimes there are just less expensive alternative brands that sell similar items at a lower price. Apple had just about cornered the music player market for a while. But during the iPod craze Microsoft offered a product called a Zune and Creative Labs offered a series of players under the Zen product line at a much lower price point. Apple's products were great but considering they were also the most expensive, my wife and I opted for Zen players instead. We loved them and got years of great use from them without having to pay top dollar. While I typically use my smart phone these days for music, those Zen players still work and are still available for an afternoon run.

There is always another brand offering a similar product for less. That is just the way our economy works. Sometimes the cheaper brand offers a product of very similar quality, other times the lower price truly means lower quality. In those instances it can be helpful to know where to find name brand products that simply cost less. Thankfully there are a few stores that specialize in just that! Retailers such as TJ Max, Payless and Tuesday Morning all purchase overstock items from other retailers and sell them at a discounted price. This can include a wide variety of items, but usually includes brands that may otherwise be out of your budget. By shopping at these discount stores, some of the higher quality, name brand items can be found at generic brand prices.

When considering a vacation, simply scheduling at the right time can provide a discount. Last minute deals can be found when providers have empty seats or rooms to fill so if you are flexible and open to looking at last minute deals, this could be a great option. On the other end of the spectrum would be preplanning way in advance. By planning a trip early, you lock in rates before the peak season demand kicks in, therefore getting a vacation at a reduced price.

Speaking of timing, simply planning a vacation off season can save quite a bit. This means planning to go to a location at a time of year when most people don't travel there. This could include vacationing in the mountains in summer for bike riding or hiking rather than winter for skiing. Even planning on a timeframe when most kids are in school will help because it is more difficult for families to travel when their kids are supposed to be in class.

When all else fails, the best way to save vacation money is to take a "staycation". This term has become popular recently but it really just means taking time off of work and staying at home. Obviously this saves all of the cost that travel would have incurred so it is great on a bank account. While the idea might sound boring since aren't heading out to exotic places, try looking into tourism in your area. Many people tend to ignore the tourist style activities available in their home towns simply because they assume there must not be anything fun to do near home. But all cities have at least something of interest. By acting like a tourist and looking for those hidden local gyms, you can have a very exciting staycation.

Insurance has been touched on a few times throughout this book but there are few additional money saving tidbits I can provide. Most insurance providers I have worked with offer some kind of multi policy discount. By insuring more than one car, motorcycle, boat, RV, etc. with them, they provide an overall discount on all of the policies. If you have recently been married and still have separate policies, consider combining them to receive a discount of this sort. If you stay with a company for several years, another discount usually appears. This could be in the form of a vanishing deductible, a loyalty discount or an accident free premium decrease if you did not file any claims. In any of those cases, picking a carrier and sticking with them will reduce your overall cost over time.

If all of the options offered so far have been used, simply try calling. Similar to the method suggested previously for credit cards, sometimes just calling a provider and asking for a discount is all it takes. They will review your account and may have special deals or price reductions based on your history.

DIY

Hiring individuals or companies to provide services is expensive since you are paying for travel time, labor time, expertise and a warranty. On the other hand trying to fix something yourself without the necessary skills could be even more costly. Thankfully many tasks around the house are fairly easy to do and can be accomplished without the fear of failure.

The easiest home DIY project has got to be painting. Anyone can dip a brush in paint and slap it on a wall. Making the splatter look nice is obviously a bit more difficult but not much. The great things about home paint projects are that they are inexpensive, do not take much time and can renew old and outdated rooms and furniture. Add to that the reuse or repurpose of items found in an attic, closet or garage and in a single weekend you could completely redecorate a room for $50 or less!

Landscaping is another easy task to accomplish without the help of a professional. While creating a beautiful design might be outside the limits of a typical non-artist, replacing overgrown bushes and flowers with something new requires only a shovel and a bit of time. Adding colorful plants and some mulch to a front flower bed will not only change the look of the landscape, it can also increase the value of your home if trying to sell. Never underestimate the value of drive up appeal.

There are a few other home repairs that will feel less intuitive but are still great DIY projects. Minor plumbing repairs such as replacing the flapper in a toilet or unclogging a drain or outdoor tasks like replacing fence pickets are very simple to do but would cost quite a bit if a professional were hired. This brings us to the absolute best DIY tip I can provide. For almost any project you are interested in tackling, search YouTube (www.youtube.com) for a variety of how to videos. That has become my go to source for all home repair projects, as the videos are made by both professionals and other do it yourself homeowners. Since the website is free to use, you can effectively receive free training on how to reduce the cost of repairs and improvements!

DIY projects do not necessarily have to mean large repairs or improvements. Think back to childhood when making birdhouses, necklaces or other crafts was a common occurrence. There are retailers dedicated to the sale of home craft supplies that can spur imagination and provide hours of entertainment. If you have difficulty coming up with ideas for home crafts to make, try looking at websites like Pinterest (www.pinterest.com). The site is filled with crafting ideas from others who have successfully made fun and interesting items themselves.

Several great benefits result from working on these home crafts. First, custom items tailored to your specific needs or interests are created that probably could not have been found in a store. Second, the items created are typically less expensive than a store bought alternative if one exists. Third and possibly most important is that the crafting experience can be shared with family members creating wonderful memories and strengthening relationships.

Food

Food is an important part of everyone's day to day life but that does not mean it must be expensive. Think about the meals you have had over the last week and count how many of those meals were made at home. Does the number surprise you? How many of those meals were from fast food restaurants? How many were from more expensive dine in restaurants?

It's no secret that eating out is more expensive than at home yet much more convenient because it requires no pre planning. Once again you are paying for convenience, expertise and service. The costs add up the more often you use this convenience though, so finding ways to avoid it is important. This does not necessarily have to mean cooking every meal and creating a sacked lunch each day. Even something as simple as ordering food to go from a dine-in restaurant will save you money by avoiding the cost of expensive sodas and the tip that would have been paid for service.

Thankfully cooking at home can be as easy or as complex as you want to make it. Spreading a bit of peanut butter and jelly onto a few slices of bread, then adding a few cheese cubes and an apple makes for an inexpensive, tasty and very quickly prepared meal. Spend a few minutes thinking about all of the items in your house that could work as a snack or a quick meal when combined. It is important to combine healthy items rather than just a bunch of greasy, processed food, otherwise the cost savings will just be offset by long term health issues. Check out the list below for a few items that could fit this category.

- Mixed nuts
- Cheese cubes
- Grapes
- Apples

- Oranges
- Peanut Butter
- Bread
- Crackers
- Deli meat
- Health bars
- Lettuce
- Tuna

If time allows, great tasting meals can be made in a slow cooker with very little effort. Stews, roasts and soups are very easy to make in this way. I will provide a few recipes to try in the next chapter but the great thing about making a stew or soup in a slow cooker is that creativity rewards you. By throwing in various combinations of beans, meat, liquids and vegetables a wonderful tasting meal for a family can be created. All this requires is throwing all of the items into the slow cooker then walking away for a few hours. Depending on the items used, the end result can be a full family meal for under $10.

When cooking at home, try to make meals in bulk as it provides several great benefits. First, by purchasing ingredients in bulk from a local grocer or wholesaler, they will be less expensive per ounce than the same items packaged in smaller quantities. Please note this does not work for produce, as it goes bad too quickly, so be cognizant of which items can be bought in bulk and used before deteriorating. Canned goods, dry food and anything that can be frozen are great candidates for bulk purchases. Some items like blocks of cheese can be bought in large quantities, then separated into smaller quantities and frozen. This allows you to pull out just what is needed for a period of time without having the rest go bad. In the case of a block of cheese, it can also be sliced for sandwiches, shredded for tacos or cubed for snacks. In each of those cases, buying a large block then cutting it into smaller, useable forms saves money.

Next, making meals in bulk saves time. Think about the last time you cooked at home and how much preparation, planning and actual cooking time it took. By doubling, tripling or even quadrupling that recipe, nearly the same amount of time is taken up front, but very little time is required to reheat that item the next day. Be careful with how much of a single meal you make though. Plenty of people get tired of eating the same thing over and over and that can lead to lots of waste.

Finally, when cooking in bulk is combined with proper food storage, meals could be created for an entire week or longer in just one day. My wife and I like to use disposable plastic ware containers to store food. These come in a variety of sizes to fit just about any form of meal and are inexpensive since they are intended for disposal. Some are shaped like dinner plates which can be used to prepare lunches for kids. Others are large tubs which are great for storing large quantities of stew. Regardless of the shape or size, these can store meals made in bulk, then be refrigerated for short term use or frozen for long term use. By washing and reusing them rather than disposing, these inexpensive items can be used for years.

If making meals in bulk and eating the same thing for days sound unappealing, try just storing the small amount of leftovers created each time a meal is prepared. If you manage to cook something different several nights in a row, one or two meals per week could be leftovers. By saving small portions of several different meals, leftover night will provide a variety of options rather than mass quantities of a single entrée.

Leftovers can also come from eating out. How often have you gone to a dine-in restaurant and been presented with a meal that could feed a small army? Rather than stuffing yourself so full you must be rolled out the front door, ask for a to-go box. All restaurants have them and by using them you effectively split the cost of eating out over two meals instead of just one.

The final tip I have related to saving money on food is to avoid vending machines at all cost. This is the polar opposite of buying in bulk. Vending machines provide small quantities of mostly unhealthy food at substantially inflated prices. As an alternative, carry a large bottle of water everywhere you go for an always available drink option. For food, stock some healthy snacks in a drawer at work or in your car for easy access. Items such as Clif Bars (www.clifbar.com) or nuts work great for this purpose. By following this process you will not only save money, but also have the peace of mind in knowing you have necessities conveniently available when needed.

Alcohol

Adult beverages can be delicious and can increase the fun factor of a social gathering when used appropriately. Unfortunately they also tend to inhibit judgment and can therefore lead to very large bar tabs when drinking at bars or restaurants. Over the years I have come up with a few sure fire tricks to reduce those bar tabs down to just a few dollars.

While simply staying home and making your own drinks would be the cheapest option, it is not always the most fun. If a group of friends suggests that everyone meet out somewhere for a fun filled evening, you will most likely want to tag along. In those instances try having your first drink or two at home. Please note that drinking and driving is illegal and dangerous so if you decide to drink before heading out, be sure to have a designated driver who is not drinking.

Once out, try to get to places serving alcohol during happy hour. Most restaurants and bars have a period designated in which drinks are sold at drastically reduced prices. Some hotels even offer a complimentary happy hour where drinks are free for a limited period of time. In the case of clubs or bars that charge a cover fee, that fee is usually waived during happy hour, as the time frame specified is usually very early in the evening. By taking advantage of this deal you get two discounts in one!

By following these tips, you should have had enough to drink by the time prices increase to the standard cost. If not, get another happy hour priced drink just before prices increase then sip on it for the next hour or so. At the end of the night, the entire cost of alcohol could be just a few dollars without a full priced drink ever being purchased.

Don't Cut

Since this chapter has been all about finding ways to cut costs, I think it is worth mentioning that some things should not be cut out. Sometimes cutting a cost can actually reduce a necessary benefit or could cause an even greater cost in the future.

Insurance has been mentioned several times in this book, as it is an area with significant potential for cost savings. But some people take it too far and cut out insurance altogether. Imagine getting in a car accident that was your fault and being unable to pay for repairs or even medical bills for the other party involved. Now assume you are an amazingly cautious, defensive driver and another uninsured motorist hits you. Without insurance in both cases you would be left with very large medical or repair bills.

Similarly, being underinsured for items could mean an insurance company does not pay anything when a claim is filed. Imagine the scenarios above where you are insured but only for liability. While this would pay for someone else if you caused the damage, both scenarios would mean insurance does not pay for any repairs to your vehicle. Another example of this could be if your home sits in an area known for flooding but flood insurance is not purchased. When a flood occurs, you would be left with the full responsibility of repairing a water logged home. Suddenly the cost of insurance would look very reasonable.

The previous examples have been over insuring possessions. But an even more important item to insure is your health. If a serious illness occurs and your family cannot afford a necessary procedure or medication, what happens? Even something as simple as using health insurance to receive preventative checkups can be beneficial as this process could catch conditions before they become serious. Keep things like this in mind when deciding what level to cut benefits to.

Other than insurance, there is one other item worth mentioning that can cost quite a bit over time if it is not taken advantage of. This item is a 401k plan which is offered by many employers. The idea behind it is that you contribute a portion of your pretax earnings and the company will contribute an additional amount based on your contribution. In the case of several companies I have worked for in the past, the specific calculations were something like the following.

The company will match the first 4% of your income that you choose to contribute. So if you make $10,000 and contribute 4% of it to a 401k ($400), the company will match that and contribute $400 themselves. After that, the company will match half of whatever you contribute for the next 2%. So if you make $10,000 and contribute 6% of it to a 401k ($400) the company will match the first $400 and will then also provide half of the rest which would be another $100 for a total of $500. In this scenario, by not contributing the full $600, you would miss free money available from your employer.

Benefits vary from company to company and your specific scenario may differ from that specified in my example. But knowing where cuts will cost you, where they will prevent free money and where the cost of cutting is greater than the short term savings is very important. By spending wisely and cutting only where necessary all of the pieces of your financial puzzle will start to fall into place.

20 – Recipes

As mentioned previously, a great way to save money is to eat at home instead of fast food or out at nice restaurants. For those without cooking experience, that's easier said than done. This chapter will contain a series of easy recipes that can be created cheaply while providing a large amount of tasty food.

One comment I hear quite often is that food at restaurants tastes much better than anything made at home. To challenge that mindset I have thrown a few extremely tasty desserts into the mix that I believe are better than anything I have ever eaten at a restaurant. Try each of them and see what you think.

Also, since you are reading this book to learn and grow, I highly recommend experimenting with these recipes. To assist in that I have added an area labeled "Notes:" below each recipe where you can add your own personalized comments for future improvements. Use this to improve on each recipe every time one is made and after a few iterations each will be perfectly tailored to your own personal taste. From there you can pass them on to a friend or relative for them to enjoy!

Pulled Pork (slow cooker)

Ingredients:

> 3 – 4 pounds of pork shoulder
> 2 tablespoons crushed garlic
> 1 – 2 tablespoons liquid smoke
> 1 teaspoon salt (optional)
> 2 cups beef broth

Instructions:

1. Put all ingredients into a large crock pot.
2. Cook for either 4 hours on high or 8 hours on low until it falls apart when poked with a fork.
3. Every 2 hours, use a spoon to ladle some of the liquid over the pork shoulder to keep it from drying out.
4. When the pork is finished cooking, pull it out onto a plate and shred it using 2 forks. Serve by itself, with barbecue sauce or on a bun.

Notes:

Stew (slow cooker)

Ingredients:

> 2 pounds of beef (chuck roast, ground, etc)
> 1 chopped onion
> 4 chopped carrots
> 4 chopped potatoes
> 4 chopped celery stalks
> 1 can of corn
> 2 tablespoons crushed garlic
> 1 bay leaf
> 3 cups beef broth
> ½ cup of your favorite red wine
> 1 small can of tomato paste
> 1 teaspoon salt
> 1 teaspoon pepper

Instructions:

1. Preheat oven to 450 degrees.
2. Brown the beef in a skillet.
3. Add the beef and all other ingredients except the wine to the slow cooker.
4. Cook on high for 4 hours or low for 8 hours.
5. Every 2 hours, use a spoon to stir the stew.
6. 30 minutes before the stew is finished, add the wine.
7. Serve in a bowl with a side of garlic toast for a delicious meal.

Notes:

Chili (slow cooker)

Ingredients:

> 2 lbs ground beef
> 1 large can diced tomatoes
> 1 can of Rotel
> 1 chopped onion
> 1 chopped bell pepper
> 4 cans of beans (un-drained kidney, great northern, pinto or other bean)
> 1 teaspoon garlic salt
> ½ teaspoon salt
> 1 teaspoon cumin
> 5 tablespoons chili powder
> 2-3 bay leaves
> Dash of paprika
> Dash of pepper

Instructions:

1. Brown the beef in a skillet.
2. Add the beef and all other ingredients to the slow cooker.
3. Cook on high for 4 hours or low for 8 hours.
4. Every 2 hours, use a spoon to stir the chili.
5. Serve either by itself, topped with cheese and sour cream or ladle over corn chips.

Notes:

Chicken and Rice (oven)

Ingredients:

> 1 (10.75 ounce) can Condensed Cream of Mushroom Soup
> 1 cup chicken broth
> 1 cup uncooked regular long-grain rice (not instant)
> 1/4 teaspoon paprika
> 1/4 teaspoon ground black pepper
> 1/4 teaspoon garlic powder
> 4 skinless, boneless chicken breasts
> Optionally add peas and carrots to the rice

Instructions:

1. Preheat oven to 375 degrees.
2. Mix soup, water, rice, paprika, black pepper and garlic in 2-quart shallow baking dish.
3. Top with chicken.
4. Season the chicken with additional paprika, pepper and garlic powder if desired.
5. Cover with foil.
6. Bake at 375 degrees for 45 minutes or until done.

Notes:

Kabobs (grill)

Ingredients:

 1 pound chicken breast
 1 bell pepper
 1 onion
 3 potatoes
 Gordon's Grub Rub ®
 Metal skewers

Instructions:

1. Preheat grill to around 400 degrees.
2. Cut the chicken into 1" cubes.
3. Cut the onion into 1" squares.
4. Cut the bell pepper into 1" squares.
5. Cut the potatoes into 1" cubes.
6. Season the chicken to taste with Gordon's Grub Rub ®
7. Add one bell pepper square to a skewer followed by one onion, then a cube of chicken and a potato cube.
8. Continue alternating the items until the skewer has 1" to spare on each end. Do the same on additional skewers until the ingredients have all been used.
9. Wrap each skewer in foil.
10. Set grill to medium heat and place skewers wrapped in foil on the grill for 10 minutes.
11. Un-wrap all skewers and put them back on the grill for another 10 minutes or until fully cooked.

Notes:

Burgers (grill)

Ingredients:

1 pound ground beef
1 teaspoon ground black pepper
1 teaspoon seasoned salt
1 teaspoon garlic powder
1 teaspoon onion powder

Instructions:

1. Preheat grill to around 400 degrees.
2. Divide the ground beef into 3 or 4 patties.
3. Sprinkle half of the seasoned salt, pepper, garlic powder and onion powder on one side of the patties.
4. Flip the patties.
5. Sprinkle the rest of the seasonings on the other side of the patties.
6. Set grill heat to medium.
7. Cook patties for 6-8 minutes depending on how well done you want the burgers to be.
8. Flip the patties and cook for an additional 6-8 minutes.

Notes:

Flavored Popcorn (microwave)

Ingredients:

> 3 tablespoons of popcorn kernels
> 1 brown paper sack
> Spray butter
> Butter flavored seasoned salt (or other popcorn seasoning)

Instructions:

1. Place the 3 tablespoons of popcorn kernels into the brown paper sack.
2. Cook the kernels in a microwave for no more than 2 minutes. Please note popcorn burns easily so depending on your microwave the time might need to be reduced to 1 minute and 30 seconds.
3. Dump ¼ of the bag of cooked popcorn into a large bowl and spray 5-7 sprits of butter.
4. Sprinkle flavoring to taste.
5. Repeat steps 3-5 until all popcorn has been covered.
6. Additionally you can experiment with adding other seasonings such as parmesan, sour cream and onion or ranch.

Notes:

Cookie Sundae (microwave)

Ingredients:

> 2 tablespoon of raw cookie dough (any flavor)
> ¼ cup of ice cream (any flavor)
> Cinnamon powder (optional)
> Whipped cream (optional)
> Chocolate syrup (optional)

Instructions:

1. Place the 2 tablespoons of cookie dough into a small bowl or ramekin.
2. Cook the cookie dough in the microwave for 40-50 seconds on high. This depends on the power of your microwave so watch closely the first few times.
3. Let cool for a minute.
4. Top with ice cream.
5. Optionally top it off with a few shakes of cinnamon powder, whipped cream or chocolate syrup for additional flavor.

Notes:

Pumpkin Gingerbread (oven)

Ingredients:

> 2 cups sugar
> 1 cup brown sugar
> 1 cup vegetable oil
> 4 eggs
> 2/3 cup water
> 1 (15 ounce) can pumpkin puree
> 2 teaspoons ground ginger
> 1 teaspoon ground allspice
> 1 teaspoon ground cinnamon
> 3 1/2 cups all-purpose flour
> 2 teaspoons baking soda
> 1 1/2 teaspoons salt
> 1/2 teaspoon baking powder

Instructions:

1. Preheat oven to 350 degrees F (175 degrees C). Lightly grease two 9x5 inch loaf pans.
2. In a large mixing, combine sugar, oil and eggs; beat until smooth. Add water and beat until well blended. Stir in pumpkin, ginger, allspice and cinnamon.
3. In medium bowl, combine flour, soda, salt, and baking powder. Add dry ingredients to pumpkin mixture and blend just until all ingredients are mixed. Divide batter between prepared pans.

4. Bake in preheated oven until toothpick comes out clean, about 1 hour.

Notes:

Rum Cake (oven)

Ingredients:

> 1 (18.25 ounce) package yellow cake mix
> 1 (3.4 ounce) package instant vanilla pudding mix
> 4 eggs
> 1/2 cup water
> 1/2 cup vegetable oil
> 1/2 cup dark rum
>
> -- Glaze Topping--
> 1/4 cup milk
> 1 tsp. vanilla extract
> 2 cups powdered sugar

Instructions:

1. Preheat oven to 325 degrees F (165 degrees C).
2. Grease and flour a 10 inch Bundt pan.
3. In a large bowl, combine cake mix and pudding mix then mix in the eggs, 1/2 cup water, oil and 1/2 cup rum. Blend well.
4. Bake in the preheated oven for 60 minutes, or until a toothpick inserted into the cake comes out clean.
5. Let sit for 10 minutes in the pan then turn out onto serving plate.
6. Brush glaze over top and sides. Allow cake to absorb glaze and repeat until all glaze is used.

To make the glaze:

1. Heat milk and vanilla together over medium heat until warm.
2. Stir in sugar and whisk until smooth consistency is achieved.
3. Remove saucepan from heat and pour over cake.

Notes:

21 – Summary

Congratulations! You have reached the final chapter of Mr. Rich vs. The Joneses: Living Within Your Means. This was a big step on the path to financial stability and living within your means. With all of the information provided, you have everything necessary to become just like Mr. Rich. The choices made from here on out will determine what your future holds. Will it be continuing to keep up with the Joneses? Or will it be a mindset change, spending less than you earn and wisely saving for a bright tomorrow?

In writing this book I attempted to convey a large amount of information on a variety of topics that may or may not fit your current situation. As time goes on, that situation will change and bits that were skimmed over the first time through could become much more important. To that end I encourage you to keep this book handy as a reference in your financial adventures going forward.

To assist with your next step, I'd like to point out the single most important topic contained within this book. Without it, any attempt at financial security is sure to fail, but with it anything is possible. That most important tip is simply to spend less than you earn. This is the definition of living within your means and should be a staple in the strategy used from now on.

While I covered the basics and even delved deeper into many topics, there is always more to learn. If you are interested in continuing your education, I highly suggest reading any financial articles on your favorite news website as they change regularly. A few of my favorites are CNN (www.cnn.com), Yahoo (www.yahoo.com) and MSNBC (www.msnbc.com). Searching online for topics such as "saving strategies", "living within your means" or even just "retirement" can provide a wealth of valuable information as well. Each writer has their own opinions and the correct path for you will most likely be a combination of ideas from several sources.

Once you have all of these basic ideas down, I encourage you to also look into retirement strategies. While that topic was vaguely touched upon, it was beyond the scope of this book and could easily warrant its own book. That said, it is a very important topic to learn as plenty of Americans are underprepared and will therefore need to work longer rather than retire.

That wraps up the tips and strategies I have to offer. Thank you for taking the time to learn a bit from my experience, I hope you have enjoyed it. Good luck on the path to Living Within Your Means and remember when you see everyone else doing something that doesn't make sense, it might be wise to do the opposite.

Appendix A

Forms & Formulas

On the following pages you will find a collection of all of the forms and formulas contained within the chapters of this book. I will also include a few additional items that may be of use on your path to living like Mr. Rich.

Forms

Budget	
Expense	**Amount**
Mortgage #1	
Mortgage #2	
Home Phone	
Cell Phone	
Internet	
TV	
Auto Loan	
Auto Insurance	
Electricity - Utility	
Gas - Utility	
Water - Utility	
Gym Membership	
Website Subscriptions	
Gas - Auto	
Groceries	
Fast Food	
Life Insurance	
Homeowner's Association Dues	
Medical Prescriptions	
Cigarettes	
Alcohol	
TOTAL	$

Great Value	Not A Value

Weekly Menu Planner

Sunday	Monday
Tuesday	Wednesday
Thursday	Friday
Saturday	Notes

Weekly Menu Planner With Shopping List

Sunday
_____
_____
_____

Monday
_____
_____
_____

Tuesday
_____
_____
_____

Wednesday
_____
_____
_____

Thursday
_____
_____
_____

Friday
_____
_____
_____

Saturday
_____
_____
_____

Net Worth Form

Assets		Liabilities	
Cash	$	Auto Loan	$
Checking	$	Mortgage #1	$
Savings	$	Mortgage #2	$
CD	$	Personal Loan	$
Mutual Funds	$	Credit Card #1	$
401k	$	Credit Card #2	$
IRA	$	Installment Debt	$
Roth IRA	$		$
Car	$		$
House	$		$
	$		$
	$		$
	$		$
	$		$
	$		$
	$		$
	$		$
	$		$
	$		$
	$		$
	$		$
	$		$
	$		$
	$		$
	$		$
	$		$
Total	$	Total	$

Total Assets – Total Liabilities = Net Worth

Formulas

Budget calculation

    INCOME (after taxes) – EXPENSES = Extra/Shortfall

Net worth calculations

    ASSETS – LIABILITIES = NET WORTH

    What you own – what you owe = what you're worth

Compound interest calculation (monthly)

    $CV = P(1 + r/n)^n$

    CV = Current Value

    P = Principal Investment

    r = monthly interest rate or the annual interest rate divided by 100

    n = number of months

Loan calculation

$$MP = P * (r(1+r)^n / (1+r)^n - 1)$$

MP = Monthly Payment

P = Principal

r = monthly interest rate; annual interest rate divided by 100 then divided by 12

n: number of months or number of total payments

Total loan cost calculation

Monthly Payment * Number of Months = Total Loan Cost

Total Loan Cost – Purchase Price = Amount paid in interest

Appendix B

Important Links

Quite a few links to websites were provided throughout this book. In order to ease your transition into a future of ongoing research and living within your means, I have gathered all of the links into a single location. To simplify finding a specific link, they are broken out into categories.

Video on Demand

www.netflix.com

www.hulu.com

www.comedycentral.com

www.nbc.com

www.youtube.com

Music on Demand

www.pandora.com

www.rdio.com

Discount Shopping

www.ebay.com

www.craigslist.org

Informational

www.wikipedia.org

www.transunion.com

www.experian.com

www.equifax.com

www.pinterest.com

Online Retailers

www.amazon.com

www.gamestop.com

Retailers

www.sea-doo.com

www.harley-davidson.com

www.apple.com

www.craftsman.com

www.brita.com

Service Providers

www.realtor.com

www.angieslist.com

www.discovercard.com

Products

www.lego.com

www.brita.com

www.leapfrog.com

www.furby.com

www.ty.com

www.hasbro.com

www.clifbar.com

Coupons

www.groupon.com

www.coupons.com

www.valpak.com

www.retailmenot.com

Software

http://www.google.com/docs/about/

www.openoffice.org

http://www.adobe.com/products/photoshop.html

www.getpaint.net

www.gimp.org

www.gmail.com

mail.yahoo.com

www.outlook.com

News

www.cnn.com

www.yahoo.com

www.msnbc.com

About the Author

J.J. Logan has been in the IT industry for over 15 years, has a Bachelor of Science in Information Systems and is a Microsoft Certified Solutions Developer. He is also a loving husband, father of 2 and spent his childhood learning from a mother with a PhD in Psychology. This has lead to a detail oriented life of self reflection and analysis as well as an acute awareness of the responsibility family life requires.

These factors have all contributed to J.J.'s interest in learning and analyzing financial patterns in the environment around him. This information has allowed him to tailor a financial lifestyle that breaks from the norm yet produces a stability few get to experience. All of this knowledge has now been wrapped up in his new book Mr. Rich vs. The Joneses: Living Within Your Means.

www.ingramcontent.com/pod-product-compliance
Lightning Source LLC
Chambersburg PA
CBHW051458170526
45166CB00001B/289